MERRY CHRISTMAS

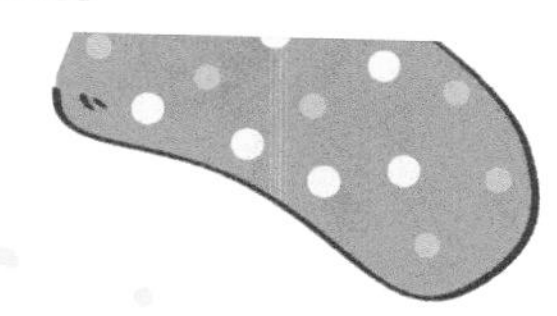

15 easy amigurumi patterns

CROCHET GNOMES

Original crochet patterns, text and photos by Maria Ermolova
© 2022 First published. All rights reserved.

No part of this publication may be reproduced, stored in a retrieval system or transmitted in any form or by any means without the prior written permission of the publisher and copyright owner.

The book is sold subject to the condition that all designs are copyright and are not for commercial or educational reproduction without the permission of the designer and copyright owner.

The publisher and authors can accept no legal responsibility for any consequences arising from the application of information, advice or instructions given in this publication.

Gnomes know a lot of things. For example, they know how to select the tastiest of two mushrooms if asked to choose. They can predict the weather simply by touching a mouse's skin or smelling leaves that have fallen to the ground. They know how to talk a hungry fox out of stealing the last egg. But best of all, perhaps, they know that Christmas lasts only for as long as we want it to. Why is that? It's because Christmas begins when we start preparing for it.

A magical feeling of expectation and anticipation. When you can already picture a Christmas tree sparkling with lights and surrounded by gifts and can even smell the gingerbread cookies and magic in the air.

Let this winter play out like a fairy tale. Let it smell like chocolate and sound like a violin. Be sure to warm yourself up with a comfy blanket and a cup of hot cocoa while finding time to surround yourself with nice movies and books, pleasant company, and crochet projects.

Grab some yarn and a crochet hook and give yourself a little taste of Christmas. This is an invitation for you to make some happy gnomes who know a lot. And the best part is that they will know the warmth and skill of your hands as well as the light and love that live in your heart.

If you put a gnome in your kitchen, he will always make sure that the table is filled with food and that your home never experiences a shortage of food...

In the bedroom, the gnome will protect family happiness and sweet dreams.

If you want for your home to always be eagerly visited by friends and good people, put a little gnome in your living room.

If you want a lot of Christmas presents, let the gnomes sit under your Christmas tree.

If you want to share emotions with people dear to you, give them gnomes that are linked to your magical hands.

Basic Christmas Gnome
Page 9
Basic Christmas Gnome With Holly Leaves
Page 17
Gentleman
Page 21
Snowman
Page 27
Xmas Flower Stripes
Page 47
Gingerbread
Page 33
Christmas Gnome with stripes
Page 41
Reindeer Gnome
Page 55

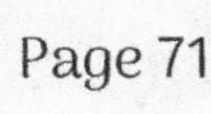

Recommendations

Stitch guides find on page 106

Yarn

Blend: cotton and acrylic fiber yarn
Yarn Weight: Sport / Fine
Yarn length/weight: approx. 160meters (174 yds) per 50gram ball.
Yarn ideas: YarnArt Jeans (used for designs from this book), Scheepjes Softfun, Sirdar Snuggly Replay DK.

If you are going to use different from the required yarn, you need to grab a crochet hook that suitable for your yarn and gauge/tension should be tight enough, so the toy stuffing doesn't show up through the crocheted fabric.

Tools

Recommended Hook in Metric Size Range: 2.5mm
Stitch markers x3

Gauge/Tension

Rd 1	6SC in magic ring, tighten the ring [6]
Rd 2	INC in each st around [12]
Rd 3	*(SC in next st, INC in next st)from*rep x6 [18]
Rd 4	*(SC in next st, INC in next st, SC in next st) from*rep x6 [24]
Rd 5	*(SC in next 3sts, INC in next st) from*rep x6 [30]
Rd 6	*(SC in next 2sts, INC in next st, SC in next 2sts) from*rep x6 [36]
	Size: Ø4.5-5cm If you are going to use different from the required yarn, you need to grab a crochet hook that is suitable for your yarn, and the gauge/ tension should be tight enough, so the toy stuffing doesn't show up through the crocheted fabric

Tips before you start

Single Crochet "V" and "X"

The typical method to make a single crochet is to insert your hook into a stitch, yarn over, pull through, yarn over, pull through both loops. This method makes a 'V' stitch.

The other lesser-known method to make a single crochet is to insert your hook into a stitch, yarn under, pull through, yarn over, pull through both loops. This method makes an 'X' stitch. Please, note that I use SC "x".

Scan for the video tutorial

Lifehack

You can use this crocheted item as a door stop.

Make a small fabric bag (a size 10cm x 15cm or so) (as well you can use a finished small pouch bag and stitch along an opening when a bag is filled with some filler).

Fill with Pebbles, cat litter, washed sand, rice or beans (food may attract insects).

When you have done a first round with decrease at a bottom of each gnome you can put the bag inside along with the rest of the filler and continue crocheting closing the bottom.

Basic Christmas Gnome

SIZE: 26 cm / 10 in

	COLOR AND YARN	TOTAL FOR A PROJECT
Red	★ Yarn Art Jeans 90	Approx. 40g/140meters
White	Yarn Art Jeans 62	Approx. 12g/40meters
Wheat	★ Yarn Art Jeans 05	Approx. 10g/35meters
Light Green	★ Yarn Art Jeans 29	Approx. 5g/17meters

OTHER MATERIALS

- Stuffing approx. 50g

CROCHET STICHES:

Ch, SC, hdc, DC, INC, sl st, SC2tog, FLO, BLO

Use a contrast thread to mark the beginning of each round. Do not remove it until your work is completed.

STEP 1 HAT

Rd 1	**Red**: 6SC in magic ring, tighten the ring [6]
Rd 2	SC in each st around [6]
Rd 3	*(SC in next st, INC in next st)from*rep x3 [9]
Rd 4	SC in each st around [9]
Rd 5	*(SC in next st, INC in next st, SC in next st) from*rep x3 [12]
Rd 6	SC in each st around [12]
Rd 7	*(SC in next st, INC in next st, SC in next st) from*rep x4 [16]
Rd 8-9	SC in each st around [16]
Rd 10	*(SC in next 3sts, INC in next st)from*rep x4 [20]
Rd 11-12	SC in each st around [20]
Rd 13	*(SC in next 2sts, INC in next st, SC in next 2sts) from*rep x4 [24]
Rd 14-15	SC in each st around [24]
Rd 16	*(SC in next 5sts, INC in next st)from*rep x4 [28]
Rd 17-18	SC in each st around [28]
Rd 19	*(SC in next 3sts, INC in next st, SC in next 3sts) from*rep x4 [32]
Rd 20-21	SC in each st around [32]
Rd 22	*(SC in next 7sts, INC in next st)from*rep x4 [36]
Rd 23-24	SC in each st around [36]
Rd 25	*(SC in next 4sts, INC in next st, SC in next 4sts) from*rep x4 [40]
Rd 26-27	SC in each st around [40]
Rd 28	*(SC in next 9sts, INC in next st)from*rep x4 [44]
Rd 29-30	SC in each st around [44]
Rd 31	*(SC in next 5sts, INC in next st, SC in next 5sts) from*rep x4 [48]
Rd 32-33	SC in each st around [48]
Rd 34	*(SC in next 11sts, INC in next st)from*rep x4 [52]
Rd 35-36	SC in each st around [52]
Rd 37	*(SC in next 6sts, INC in next st, SC in next 6sts) from*rep x4 [56]
Rd 38	SC in each st around [56]

CONTINUE: BODY

Rd 39	SC BLO in each st around [56]
Rd 40	SC in next 12sts, SC BLO in next 4sts(here we will attach the arm), SC in next 24sts, SC BLO in next 4sts(here we will attach the arm), SC in next 12sts [56]
Rd 41-45	SC in each st around [56]
Rd 46	*(SC in next 13sts, INC in next st)from*rep x4 [60]
Rd 47-50	SC in each st around [60]
Rd 51	*(SC in next 7sts, INC in next st, SC in next 7sts) from*rep x4 [64]
Rd 52-53	SC in each st around [64]
Rd 54	*(SC in next 3sts, SC2tog, SC in next 3sts) from*rep x8 [56]
Rd 55-57	SC in each st around [56]
Rd 58	*(SC in next 5sts, SC2tog)from*rep x8 [48]
	Stuff
Rd 59-60	SC in each st around [48]
Rd 61	SC BLO in each st around [48]
Rd 62	*(SC in next 2sts, SC2tog, SC in next 2sts) from*rep x8 [40]
Rd 63	*(SC in next 3sts, SC2tog)from*rep x8 [32]
Rd 64	*(SC in next st, SC2tog, SC in next st) from*rep x8 [24]
Rd 65	*(SC in next st, SC2tog)from*rep x8 [16]
	Stuff
Rd 66	SC2tog x8 [8]
	Cut off thread and sew the opening

STEP 2 STAND

Rd 1	With a new **Red** work into stitches FLO of Rd 60 of the body: Ch1, SC FLO in each st around. (pic. 1) [48]
	Cut off thread

1

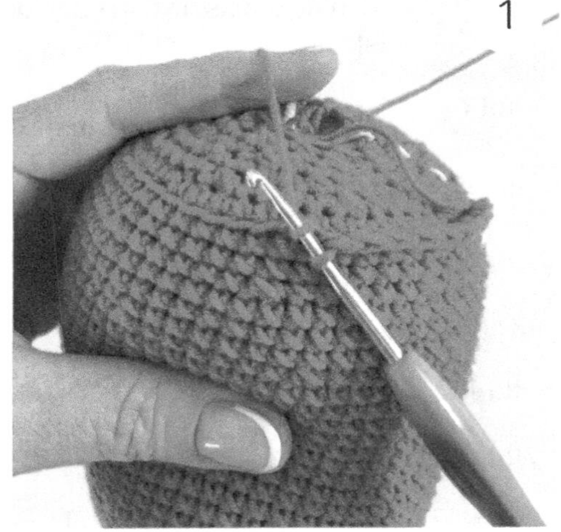

STEP 3 HAT BRIM

Rd 1	Hold the item upside down, with a new **Red** yarn work into stitches FLO of Rd 38 of the hat (pic. 2): *(SC FLO in next 13sts, INC FLO in next st)from*rep x4 [60]
Rd 2	*(SC in next 7sts, INC next st, SC in next 7sts) from*rep x4 [64]
Rd 3	*(SC in next 15sts, INC in next st)from rep x4 [68]
Rd 4	*(SC in next 8sts, INC in next st, SC in next 8sts) from*rep x4 [72]
Rd 5	sl st in each st around [72]

Cut off thread

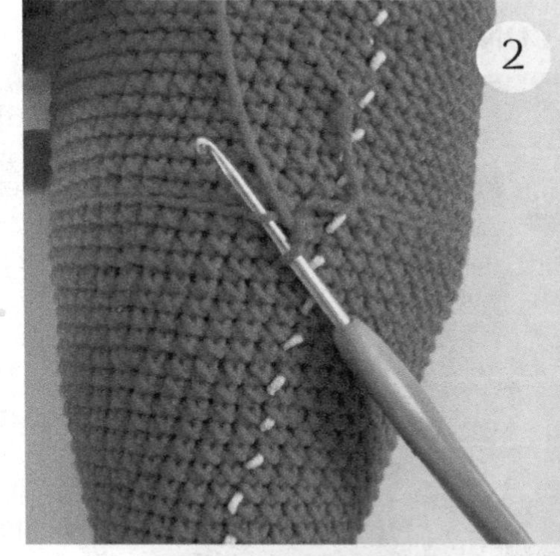

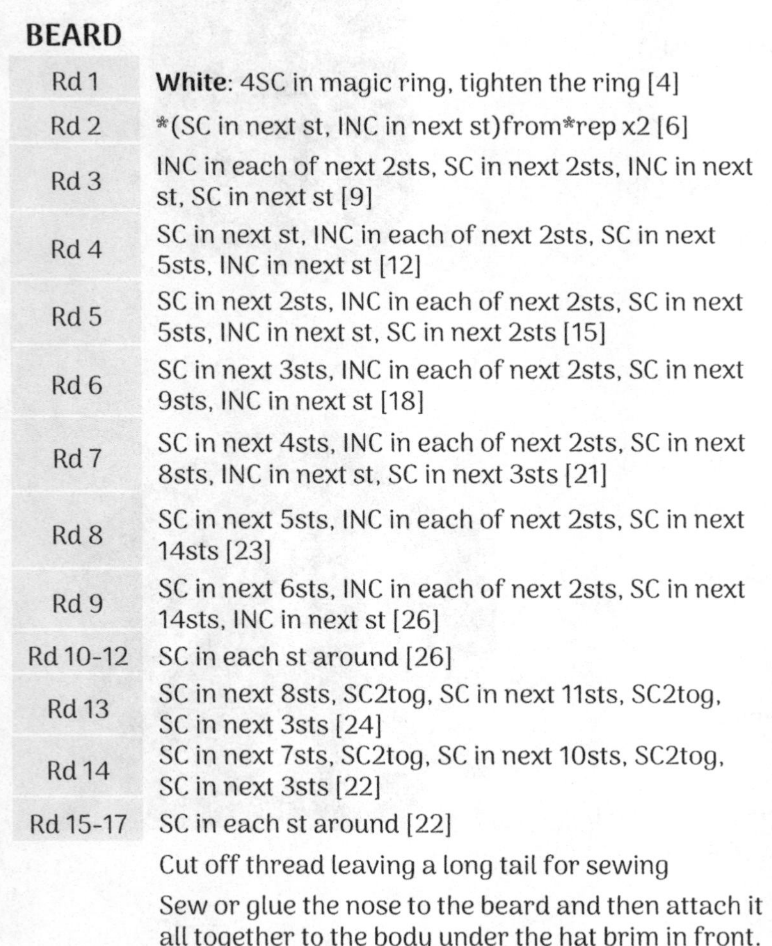

BEARD

Rd 1	**White**: 4SC in magic ring, tighten the ring [4]
Rd 2	*(SC in next st, INC in next st)from*rep x2 [6]
Rd 3	INC in each of next 2sts, SC in next 2sts, INC in next st, SC in next st [9]
Rd 4	SC in next st, INC in each of next 2sts, SC in next 5sts, INC in next st [12]
Rd 5	SC in next 2sts, INC in each of next 2sts, SC in next 5sts, INC in next st, SC in next 2sts [15]
Rd 6	SC in next 3sts, INC in each of next 2sts, SC in next 9sts, INC in next st [18]
Rd 7	SC in next 4sts, INC in each of next 2sts, SC in next 8sts, INC in next st, SC in next 3sts [21]
Rd 8	SC in next 5sts, INC in each of next 2sts, SC in next 14sts [23]
Rd 9	SC in next 6sts, INC in each of next 2sts, SC in next 14sts, INC in next st [26]
Rd 10-12	SC in each st around [26]
Rd 13	SC in next 8sts, SC2tog, SC in next 11sts, SC2tog, SC in next 3sts [24]
Rd 14	SC in next 7sts, SC2tog, SC in next 10sts, SC2tog, SC in next 3sts [22]
Rd 15-17	SC in each st around [22]

Cut off thread leaving a long tail for sewing

Sew or glue the nose to the beard and then attach it all together to the body under the hat brim in front.

NOSE

Rd 1	**Wheat**: 6SC in magic ring, tighten the ring [6]
Rd 2	INC in each st around [12]
Rd 3	*(SC in next st, INC in next st)from*rep x6 [18]
Rd 4-5	SC in each st around [18]
Rd 6	*(SC in next st, SC2tog)from*rep x6 [12]

Cut off thread leaving a long tail for sewing.

Stuff the nose a bit

ARMs

STEP 1 PALMS

Rd 1	**Wheat**: 5SC in magic ring, tighten the ring [5]
Rd 2	INC in each st around [10]
Rd 3-5	SC in each st around [10]Change to Red in last st
	Cut off Wheat
Rd 6-7	**Red**: SC in each st around [10]
Rd 8	SC BLO in each st around [10]
Rd 9-17	SC in each st around [10]

Cut off thread leaving a long tail for sewing
You can make several stitches to shape a thumb

STEP 2 CUFF

Rd 1	With **Red** work into stitches FLO of Rd 7: SC FLO in each st around [10]
Rd 2	SC in each st around [10]

Cut off thread

Sew the arms to the body under the hat brim

FLOWER #1 (Video tutorial - find below)

Rd 1	**Light Green**: 6SC in magic ring, tighten the ring [6]
Rd 2	INC in each of next 6 sts [12]; sl st into next st
Rd 3	*(Ch7, sl st in 2nd st from hook, hdc in next st of a chain, DC in next 2sts of a chain, hdc in next st of a chain, skip next st of Rd2, sl st in next st of 2nd rd)from*rep x6

Cut off thread leaving a long tail for sewing

Scan for the video tutorial

FLOWER #2

Rd 1	**Red**: 6SC in magic ring, tighten the ring [6]
Rd 2	*(Ch5, sl st in 2nd st from hook, hdc in next 2sts of a chain, sl st in next st of 1st rd)from*rep x6

Cut off thread leaving a long tail for sewing

Arrange the flowers so the red flower is above the green one and stitch the flowers together with several green stitches in the middle.

TWISTED CORD

The initial thread length should be three times as long as the length of the final cord. For example, if your final cord should be approx. 50 cm, you need to grab 150 cm threads.

1. Take **Red**, **White**, **Light Green** threads approx. 150 cm length, make a knot on one end.
2. Hook on for something (I use a door handle) and start to twist.
3. Fold in half and remove the end from the door handle.
4. Straighten the cord and make a knot on the other end.

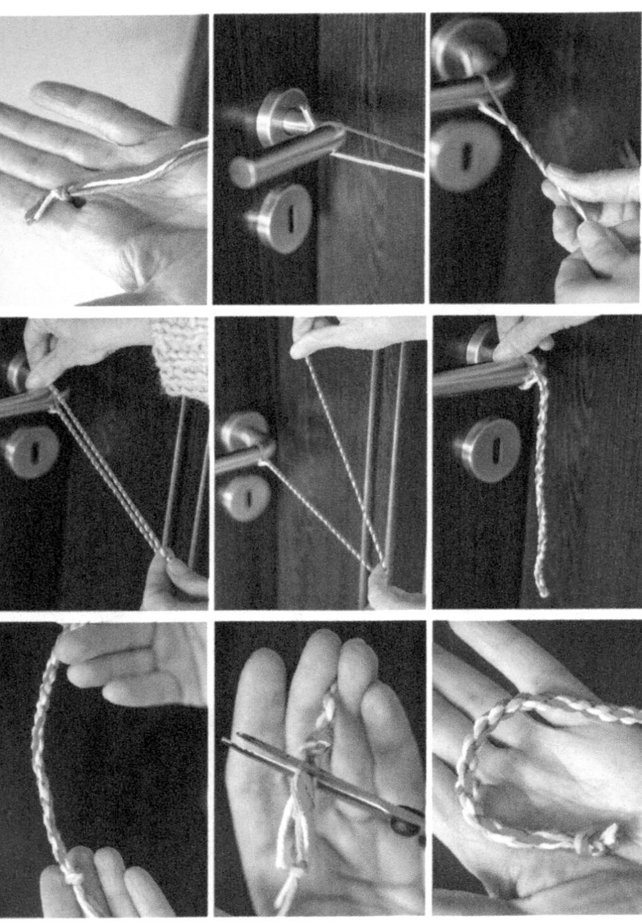

ASSEMBLING

Sew or glue the cord and the flower to the gnome's hat.

"If we take the time every day to share a little bit of warmth with those who cross our path, winter will become a little warmer. For everyone."

Basic Christmas Gnome with Holly leaves

SIZE: 26 cm / 10 in

You can decorate your basic gnome with Holly leaves.
Make 8 leaves with a dark green, and 2 with a light green.

COLOR AND YARN

Dark Green	★	Yarn Art Jeans 82
Light Green	★	Yarn Art Jeans 29

OTHER MATERIALS

- Red wooden beads Ø8mm x13

CROCHET STICHES:

Ch, SC, hdc, sl st

LEAVES

(photo tutorial see below)

Foundation chain: Chain 8

SC in 2nd st from hook, *(hdc in next 2sts, Ch2, sl st in 2nd st from hook, hdc in same st as prev hdc)from*rep x2, hdc in next st, sl st in next st, Ch2, sl st in 2nd st from hook, work into bottom of the foundation chain: *(hdc in next 2sts, Ch2, sl st in 2nd st from hook, hdc in same st as prev hdc)from*rep x2, SC in next st, sl st in next st.

Cut off thread leaving a long tail for sewing.

Scan for the video tutorial

Chain 8

SC in 2nd st from hook

hdc in next 2sts

Chain 2

Sl st in 2nd st from hook

hdc in same st as prev hdc

hdc in next 2sts

Chain 2

Sl st in 2nd st from hook

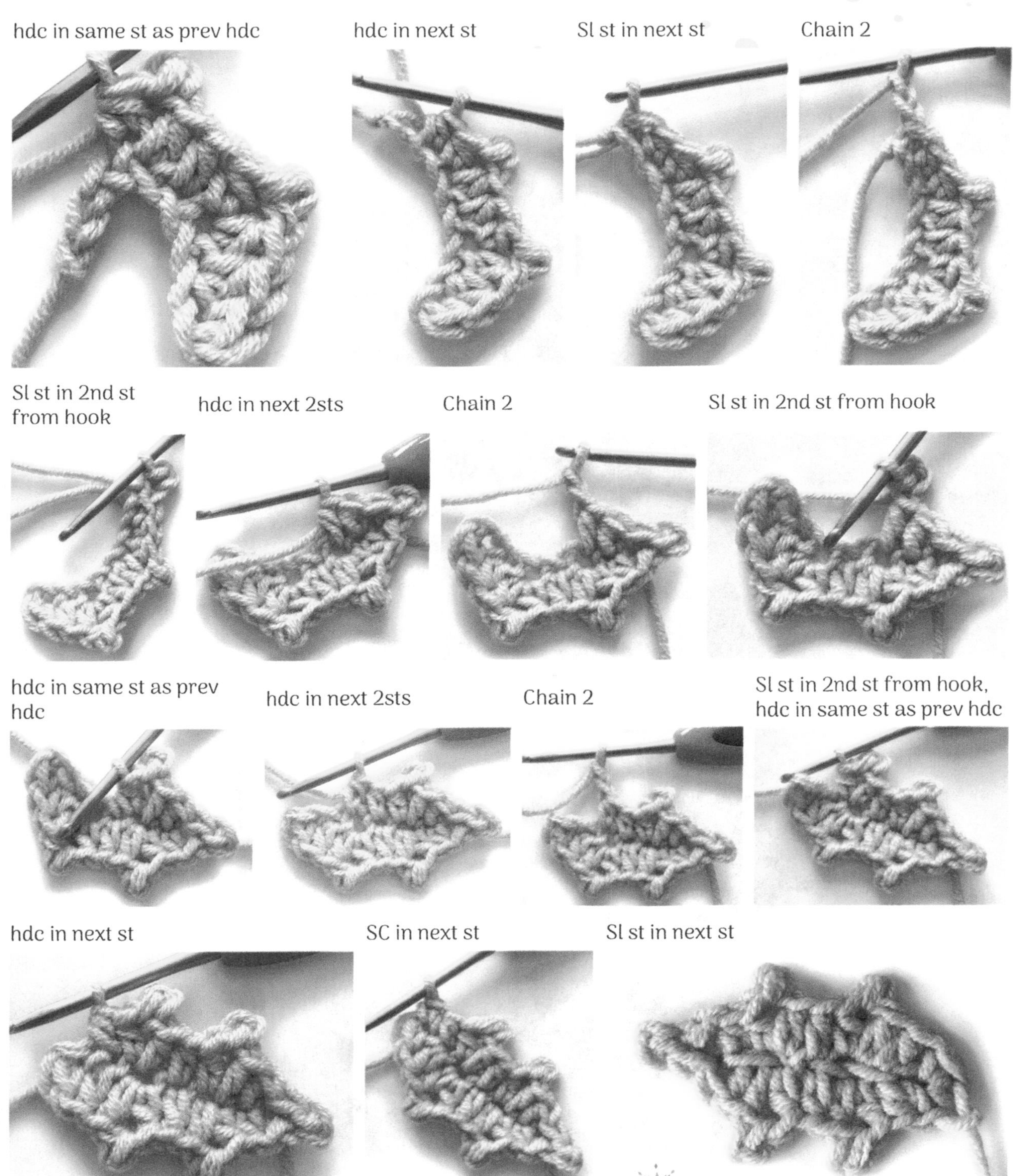
hdc in same st as prev hdc
hdc in next st
Sl st in next st
Chain 2
Sl st in 2nd st from hook
hdc in next 2sts
Chain 2
Sl st in 2nd st from hook
hdc in same st as prev hdc
hdc in next 2sts
Chain 2
Sl st in 2nd st from hook, hdc in same st as prev hdc
hdc in next st
SC in next st
Sl st in next st

Gentleman

SIZE: 17 cm / 7 in

	COLOR AND YARN	TOTAL FOR A PROJECT
Red	★ Yarn Art Jeans 90	Approx. 20g/70meters
White	Yarn Art Jeans 62	Approx. 12g/40meters
Wheat	★ Yarn Art Jeans 05	Approx. 10g/35meters
Green	★ Yarn Art Jeans 82	Approx. 20g/80meters
Yellow	★ Yarn Art Jeans 58	Approx. 5g/20meters
Black	★ Yarn Art Jeans 53	Approx. 12g/40meters

OTHER MATERIALS

- Stuffing approx. 50g
- Optional: 3 red beads Ø0.5cmg

CROCHET STICHES:

Ch, SC, hdc, DC, INC, sl st, SC2tog, FLO, BLO

Use a contrast thread to mark the beginning of each round.
Do not remove it until your work is completed.

STEP 1 HAT

Rd 1	**Black**: 6SC in magic ring, tighten the ring [6]
Rd 2	INC in each st around [12]
Rd 3	*(SC in next st, INC in next st)from*rep x6 [18]
Rd 4	*(SC in next st, INC in next st, SC in next st)from*rep x6 [24]
Rd 5	*(SC in next 3sts, INC in next st)from*rep x6 [30]
Rd 6	*(SC in next 2sts, INC in next st, SC in next 2sts)from*rep x6 [36]
	Check gauge/tension: Ø4.5-5cm
Rd 7	*(SC in next 5sts, INC in next st)from*rep x6 [42]
Rd 8	*(SC in next 3sts, INC in next st, SC in next 3sts) from*rep x6 [48]
Rd 9	*(SC in next 7sts, INC in next st)from*rep x6 [54]
Rd 10	*(SC in next 4sts, INC in next st, SC in next 4sts) from*rep x6 [60]
Rd 11	SC BLO in each st around [60]
Rd 12-25	SC in each st around [60]
Rd 26	*(SC in next 9sts, SC2tog, SC in next 9sts)from*rep x3 [57]
Rd 27	*(SC in next 17sts, SC2tog)from*rep x3 [54]
Rd 28	*(SC in next 8sts, SC2tog, SC in next 8sts)from*rep x3 [51]
Rd 29	*(SC in next 15sts, SC2tog)from*rep x3 [48]
Rd 30-32	SC in each st around [48]

STEP 2 CONTINUE: HAT BRIM

Rd 33	SC FLO in each st around [48]
Rd 34	*(SC in next 7sts, INC in next st)from*rep x6 [54]
Rd 35	*(SC in next 4sts, INC in next st, SC in next 4sts) from*rep x6 [60]
Rd 36	*(hdc in next 9sts, 2hdc in next st)from*rep x2, SC in next 9sts, INC in next st, SC in next 9sts, *(2hdc in next st, hdc in next 9sts)from*rep x2, 2hdc in last st [66]
Rd 37	*(hdc in next 5sts, 2hdc in next st, hdc in next 5sts) from*rep x2, SC in next 5sts, INC in next st, SC in next 10sts, INC in next st, SC in next 5sts, *(hdc in next 5sts, 2hdc in next st, hdc in next 5sts)from*rep x2 [72]
Rd 38	*(hdc in next 11sts, 2hdc in next st)from*rep x2, SC in next 11sts, INC in next st, SC in next 11sts, *(2hdc in next st, hdc in next 11sts)from*rep x2, 2hdc in last st [78]
Rd 39	sl st in each st around [78]
	Cut off thread

STEP 3 HAT DECORATION

Rd 1	With **Black** work into stitches FLO of the Rd 10 of the hat: SC FLO in each st around [60] Cut off thread

STEP 4 BODY

Rd 1	Grab the hat upside down, and work into stitches BLO of Rd 32 with **Red** yarn: SC BLO in each st around [48]
Rd 2	SC in next 9sts, SC BLO in next 5sts (we will attach the arm here), SC in next 6sts, SC BLO in next 8sts (we will attach the beard here), SC in next 6sts, SC BLO in next 5sts (we will attach the arm here), SC in next 9sts [48]
Rd 3	SC in each st around [48]
Rd 4	*(SC in next 7sts, INC in next st)from*rep x6 [54]
Rd 5-6	SC in each st around [54]
Rd 7	*(SC in next 4sts, INC in next st, SC in next 4sts)from*rep x6 [60]
Rd 8-11	SC in each st around [60]
Rd 12	*(SC in next 7sts, INC in next st, SC in next 7sts)from*rep x4 [64]
Rd 13-14	SC in each st around [64]
Rd 15	*(SC in next 3sts, SC2tog, SC in next 3sts)from*rep x8 [56]
Rd 16-18	SC in each st around [56]
Rd 19	*(SC in next 5sts, SC2tog)from*rep x8 [48]
Rd 20-21	SC in each st around [48]
Rd 22	SC BLO in each st around [48]
Rd 23	*(SC in next 2sts, SC2tog, SC in next 2sts)from*rep x8 [40] Stuff
Rd 24	*(SC in next 3sts, SC2tog)from*rep x8 [32]
Rd 25	*(SC in next st, SC2tog, SC in next st)from*rep x8 [24]
Rd 26	*(SC in next st, SC2tog)from*rep x8 [16] Stuff
Rd 27	SC2tog x8 [8] Cut off thread and sew the opening

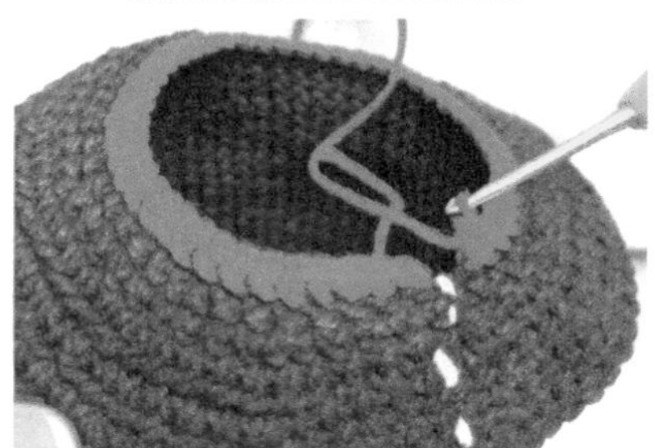

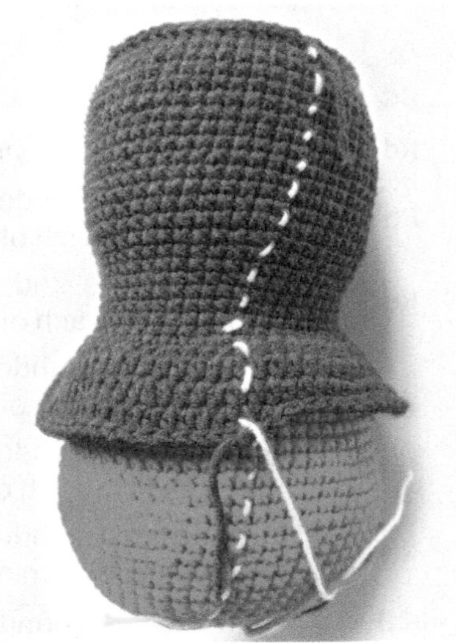

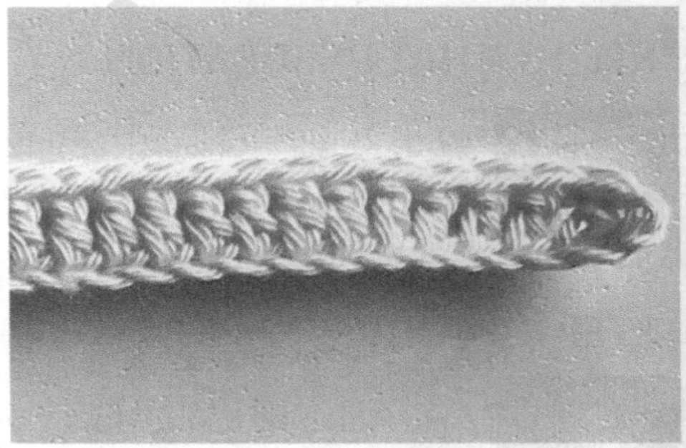

STEP 5 DECORATIVE STRAP ON THE HAT

	Yellow: Chain 52 [52]
Row 1	DC in 4th st from hook, DC in in each st across [50]
	Cut off thread leaving a long tail for sewing

STEP 6 LEAVES x2

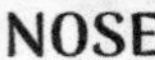

Green. Find the leave pattern on page 18. Attach (sew/glue)leaves and a strap together. You can decorate it with red beads. Attach(sew/glue) it to the hat.

NOSE

Rd 1	**Wheat**: 6SC in magic ring, tighten the ring [6]
Rd 2	INC in each st around [12]
Rd 3	*(SC in next st, INC in next st)from*rep x6 [18]
Rd 4-5	SC in each st around [18]
Rd 6	*(SC in next st, SC2tog)from*rep x6 [12]
	Cut off thread leaving a long tail for sewing
	Stuff the nose a bit

BEARD

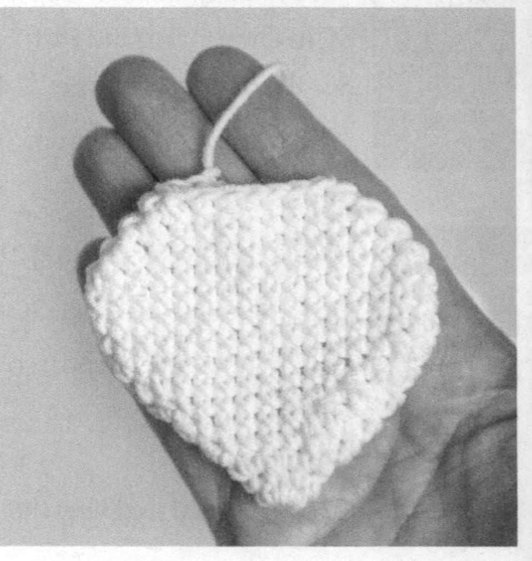

Rd 1	**White**: 6SC in magic ring, tighten the ring [6]
Rd 2	SC in each st around [6]
Rd 3	INC in each st around [12]
Rd 4	SC in next 2sts, 2hdc in each of next 2sts, SC in next 4sts, 2hdc in each of next 2sts, SC in next 2sts [16]
Rd 5	SC in next 3sts, 2hdc in each of next 2sts, SC in next 6sts, 2hdc in each of next 2sts, SC in next 3sts [20]
Rd 6	SC in next 4sts, 2hdc in each of next 2sts, SC in next 8sts, 2hdc in each of next 2sts, SC in next 4sts [24]
Rd 7	SC in next 5sts, 2hdc in each of next 2sts, SC in next 10sts, 2hdc in each of next 2sts, SC in next 5sts [28]
Rd 8	SC in next 6sts, 2hdc in each of next 2sts, SC in next 12sts, 2hdc in each of next 2sts, SC in next 6sts [32]
Rd 9-11	SC in each st around [32]

Rd 12	SC in next 6sts, SC2tog x2, SC in next 12sts, SC2tog x2, SC in next 6sts [28]
Rd 13	SC in next 5sts, SC2tog x2, SC in next 10sts, SC2tog x2, SC in next 5sts [24]
Rd 14	SC in next 4sts, SC2tog x2, SC in next 8sts, SC2tog x2, SC in next 4sts [20]
Rd 15	SC in next 3sts, SC2tog x2, SC in next 6sts, SC2tog x2, SC in next 3sts [16]
	Cut off thread leaving a long tail for sewing.
	Sew or glue the nose to the beard and then attach it all together to the body under the hat brim in front.

BOOTS

Rd 1	**Black**: 6SC in magic ring, tighten the ring [6]
Rd 2	INC each st around [12]
Rd 3	*(SC in next st, INC in next st)from*rep x6 [18]
Rd 4-6	SC in each st around [18]
Rd 7	*(SC in next st, SC2tog)from*rep x6 [12]
	Fold in half, stuff and stitch edges together by SC (SC in 6sts)
	Cut off thread leaving a long tail for sewing.
	Yellow: embroider a frame buckle
	Attach the boots to Rd 21 of the body.

ARMs

STEP 1 ARM

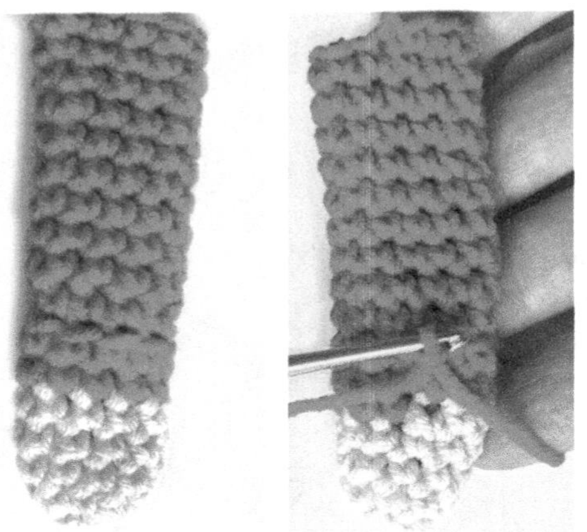

Rd 1	**Wheat**: 5SC in magic ring, tighten the ring [5]
Rd 2	INC in each st around [10]
Rd 3-5	SC in each st around [10] Change to Red in last st
	Cut off Wheat
Rd 6-7	**Red**: SC in each st around [10]
Rd 8	SC BLO in each st around [10]
Rd 9-17	SC in each st around [10]
	Cut off thread leaving a long tail for sewing

STEP 2 CUFF

Rd 1	Join **Red** to Rd 7: SC FLO in each st around [10]
Rd 2	SC in each st around [10]
	Cut off thread Sew the arms to the body under the hat brim.

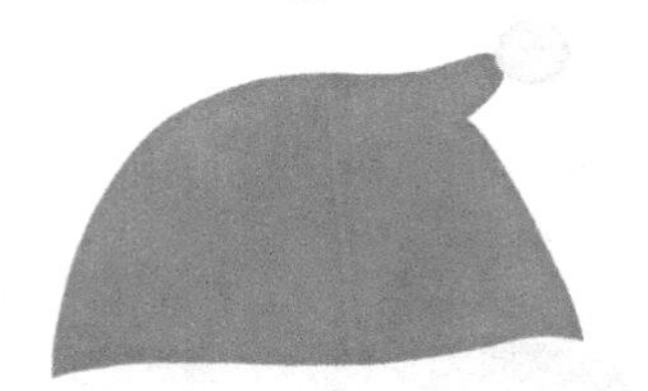

Snowman

SIZE: 17 cm / 7 in

	COLOR AND YARN	TOTAL FOR A PROJECT
Black	★ Yarn Art Jeans 53	Approx. 25g/85meters
White	Yarn Art Jeans 62	Approx. 20g/70meters
Orange	★ Yarn Art Jeans 77	Approx. 5g/20meters
Green	★ Yarn Art Jeans 29	Approx. 5g/20meters
Red	★ Yarn Art Jeans 90	Approx. 5g/20meters
Light Blue	★ Yarn Art Jeans 75	Approx. 5g/20meters
Brown	★ Yarn Art Jeans 70	Approx. 5g/20meters

OTHER MATERIALS

- Stuffing approx. 40g
- Optional: 3 white beads Ø8mm

CROCHET STICHES:

Ch, SC, hdc, INC, sl st, SC2tog, FLO, BLO

Use a contrast thread to mark the beginning of each round. Do not remove it until your work is completed.

STEP 1 HAT

Rd 1	**Black**: 6SC in magic ring, tighten the ring [6]
Rd 2	INC in each of next 6sts [12]
Rd 3	*(SC in next st, INC in next st)from*rep x6 [18]
Rd 4	*(SC in next st, INC in next st, SC in next st) from*rep x6 [24]
Rd 5	*(SC in next 3sts, INC in next st)from*rep x6 [30]
Rd 6	*(SC in next 2sts, INC in next st, SC in next 2sts) from*rep x6 [36]
	Check gauge/tension: Ø4.5-5cm
Rd 7	*(SC in next 5sts, INC in next st)from*rep x6 [42]
Rd 8	*(SC in next 3sts, INC in next st, SC in next 3sts) from*rep x6 [48]
Rd 9	*(SC in next 7sts, INC in next st)from*rep x6 [54]
Rd 10	SC BLO in each st around [54]
Rd 11-26	SC in each st around [54]
Rd 27	*(SC in next 8sts, SC2tog, SC in next 8sts) from*rep x3 [51]
 Rd 28-29	SC in each st around [51]
Rd 30	*(SC in next 15sts, SC2tog)from*rep x3 [48]
Rd 31-33	SC in each st around [48]

STEP 2 CONTINUE: HAT BRIM

Rd 34	*(SC FLO in next 7sts, INC FLO in next st)from*rep x6 [54]
Rd 35	*(SC in next 4sts, INC in next st, SC in next 4sts) from*rep x6 [60]
Rd 36	*(SC in next 9sts, INC in next st)from*rep x6 [66]
Rd 37	*(SC in next 5sts, INC in next st, SC in next 5sts) from*rep x6 [72]
Rd 38	*(SC in next 11sts, INC in next st)from*rep x6 [78]
Rd 39	sl st in each st around [78]
	Cut off thread

STEP 3 BODY

Rd 1-2	**White**. Grab a hat upside down and work into stitches BLO of Rd 33: SC BLO in each st around [48]

Rd 3-7	SC in each st around [48]
Rd 8	SC in next 11 sts, SC BLO in next 3 sts (we will attach the arm here), SC in next 20sts, SC BLO in next 3sts (we will attach the nose here), SC in next 11sts (we will attach the arm here) [48]
Rd 9	SC in each st around [48]
Rd 10	*(SC in next 7sts, INC in next st)from*rep x6 [54]
Rd 11-12	SC in each st around [54]
Rd 13	*(SC in next 4sts, INC in next st, SC in next 4sts) from*rep x6 [60]
Rd 14-15	SC in each st around [60]
Rd 16	*(SC in next 9sts, INC in next st)from*rep x6 [66]
Rd 17-20	SC in each st around [66]
Rd 21	*(SC in next 9sts, SC2tog)from*rep x6 [60]
Rd 22	SC in each st around [60]
	Stuff the hat a bit. It should not be firm
Rd 23	*(SC in next 4sts, SC2tog, SC in next 4sts) from*rep x6 [54]
Rd 24	SC in each st around [54]
Rd 25	*(SC in next 7sts, SC2tog)from*rep x6 [48]
Rd 26	SC BLO in each st around [48]
Rd 27	*(SC in next 3sts, SC2tog, SC in next 3sts) from*rep x6 [42]
	Stuff
Rd 28	*(SC in next 5sts, SC2tog)from*rep x6 [36]
Rd 29	*(SC in next 2sts, SC2tog, SC in next 2sts) from*rep x6 [30]
Rd 30	*(SC in next 3sts, SC2tog)from*rep x6 [24]
Rd 31	*(SC in next st, SC2tog, SC in next ts) from*rep x6 [18]
Rd 32	*(SC in next st, SC2tog)from*rep x6 [12]
	Stuff well
Rd 33	SC2tog x6 [6]
	Cut off thread and sew the opening

STEP 4 STAND

Rd 1	With a new **White** work into stitches FLO of Rd 25 of the body: Ch1, SC FLO in each st around [48]
	Cut off thread

NOSE

Rd 1	**Orange**: 6SC in magic ring, tighten the ring [6]
Rd 2	INC in each st around [12]
Rd 3	*(SC in next st, INC in next st)from*rep x6 [18]
Rd 4-5	SC in each st around [18]
Rd 6	*(SC in next st, SC2tog)from*rep x6 [12]
	Cut off thread leaving a long tail for sewing.
	Stuff the nose a bit. Sew or glue the nose to the body under the hat brim in front.

SCARF

	Light Blue Foundation chain: Chain 6 [6]
Row 1	SC in 2nd st from hook, SC in next 4sts [5] Ch1, Turn
Row 2-39	SC BLO in each st across [5] Ch1, Turn
Row 40	SC BLO in each st across [5]
	Cut off thread

DECORATIVE STRAP ON THE HAT

	Red Foundation chain: Chain 51 [51]
Row 1	SC in 2nd st from hook, SC in each st across [50] Ch1, Turn
Row 2	SC in each st across [50] Ch1, Turn
Row 3	sl st in each st across [50]
	Cut off thread leaving a long tail for sewing

LEAVES x2.
With Green make 2 leaves, use the leaf pattern on page 18

MITTENS+ARMs

STEP 1 MITTENS

Rd 1	**Red**: SC6 in magic ring, tighten the ring [6]
Rd 2	INC in each st around [12]
Rd 3-5	SC in each st around [12]
Rd 6	*(SC in next st, SC2tog)from*rep x4 [8]Change to Brown in last st
	Cut off Red. Stuff a bit
Rd 7	**Brown**: SC BLO in each st around [8]
Rd 8-19	SC in each st around [8]
	Cut off thread leaving a long tail for sewing

STEP 2 CUFF

	Red: Foundation chain: Chain 11 [11]
Row 1	hdc in 2nd st from hook, hdc in next 9sts [10]
	Attach the cuff to the arm

STEP 3 THUMB

	Red: Embroider a thumb with several stitches

Sew the arms to the body leaving a space for a scarf. Sew or glue leaves to the red hat strap. You can decorate it with white beads and then attach it to the hat.
Tie the scarf on your snowman.

Gingerbread

SIZE: 28 cm / 11 in

	COLOR AND YARN	TOTAL FOR A PROJECT
Off-white	Yarn Art Jeans 03	Approx. 15g/55meters
Brown	★ Yarn Art Jeans 40	Approx. 30g/105meters
Honey caramel	★ Yarn Art Jeans 07	Approx. 20g/70meters
Wheat	★ Yarn Art Jeans 05	Approx. 10g/35meters
White	Yarn Art Jeans 62	Approx. 7g/25meters

OTHER MATERIALS

- Stuffing approx. 50g
- Optional: x3 green beads Ø8mm; x4 red beads Ø11mm

CROCHET STICHES:

Ch, SC, hdc, DC, INC, sl st, SC2tog, FLO, BLO, Surface slip stitch

ADDITIONAL TOOLS:

Stitch markers x3

Use a contrast thread to mark the beginning of each round. Do not remove it until your work is completed.

Scan to watch video for Rd 1-21

STEP 1 HAT (icing topping)

Rd 1	**Off-white**: 4SC in magic ring, tighten the ring [4]
Rd 2	*(SC in next st, INC in next st)from*rep x2 [6]
Rd 3-4	SC in each st around [6]
Rd 5	INC in each of next 2sts, SC in next 2sts, INC in next st, SC in next st [9]
Rd 6	SC in each st around [9]
Rd 7	SC in next st, INC in each of next 2sts, SC in next 5sts, INC in next st [12]
Rd 8	SC in each st around [12]
Rd 9	SC in next 2sts, INC in each of next 2sts, SC in next 5sts, INC in next st, SC in next 2sts [15]
Rd 10	SC in each st around [15]
Rd 11	SC in next 3sts, INC in each of next 2sts, SC in next 9sts, INC in next st [18]
Rd 12	SC in each st around [18]
Rd 13	SC in next 4sts, INC in each of next 2sts, SC in next 8sts, INC in next st, SC in next 3sts [21]
Rd 14	SC in each st around [21]
Rd 15	SC in next 5sts, INC in each of next 2sts, SC in next 14sts [23]
Rd 16	SC in next 6sts, INC in each of next 2sts, SC in next 14sts, INC in next st [26]
Rd 17	SC in each st around [26]
	SC in next 3sts, sl st (place a stitch marker #1 in the same stitch as sl st), Turn
	SC in 2nd st from hook, SC in next 2sts, (don't forget to put here your contrast thread-beginning of round), SC in next 10sts, sl st in next st (place a stitch marker #2 in same stitch as sl st), Turn
	SC in 2nd st from hook, SC in next 9sts. Do not turn
Rd 18	SC in next 3sts, SC in stitch with a stitch marker #1, SC in next 11sts, SC in stitch with a stitch marker #2, SC in next 10sts [26]
Rd 19	SC in next 2sts, INC in next st, SC in next 4sts, INC in each of next 2sts, SC in next 7sts, INC in next st, SC in next 9sts [30]
Rd 20	SC FLO in next 3sts, hdc FLO in next 2sts, SC FLO in next 13sts, hdc FLO in next 2sts, DC FLO in next 7sts, hdc FLO in next st, SC FLO in next 2sts [30]
Rd 21	SC in next 3sts, 2hdc in next st, SC in next 14 sts, hdc in next 2sts, DC in next 3sts, 2DC in next st, DC in next 3sts, hdc in next st, SC in next 2sts [32]
	Drop a loop (we will use it on STEP 3). Go to STEP 2

STEP 2 HAT – COOKIE DOUGH

Rd 1	**Brown**: work into stitches BLO of Rd 19 of STEP 1: SC BLO in each st around [30]
Rd 2	*(SC in next 5sts, INC in next st)from*rep x5 [35]
Rd 3-4	SC in each st around [35]
Rd 5	*(SC in next 3sts, INC in next st, SC in next 3sts) from*rep x5 [40]
Rd 6-7	SC in each st around [40]
Rd 8	*(SC in next 7sts, INC in next st)from*rep x5 [45]
Rd 9-11	SC in each st around [45]
	(place a stitch marker #1 into the last stitch of Rd 11)
Rd 12	*(SC BLO in next 4sts, INC BLO in next st, SC BLO in next 4sts)from*rep x5 [50]
Rd 13-15	SC in each st around [50]
	(place a stitch marker #2 into the last stitch of Rd 15)
Rd 16	*(SC BLO in next 9sts, INC BLO in next st) from*rep x5 [55]
Rd 17-19	SC in each st around [55]
	(place a stitch marker #3 into the last stitch of Rd 19)
Rd 20	*(SC BLO in next 5sts, INC BLO in next st, SC BLO in next 5sts)from*rep x5 [60]
Rd 21-23	SC in each st around [60]
Rd 24	SC FLO in each st around [60]
	Drop a loop, Do not cut off Brown, We will use this thread on STEP 4

STEP 3 ICING DRIPS

Get back to STEP 1 where we left **Off-white**:
Continue: make drips:

Rd 1

The first drip is based on a foundation chain 5: Chain 5, hdc in 2nd Ch from hook, hdc in each st of chain, hdc in stitch of main part where Ch5 comes from, skip next st of a main part,(Photo tutorial on page 65). Now work SC in next 1-3 sts of the main part to separate drips

The same way we make drips based on different foundation chain lengths and make different number of SC between drips to separate them.

Cut off thread leaving a long tail for sewing

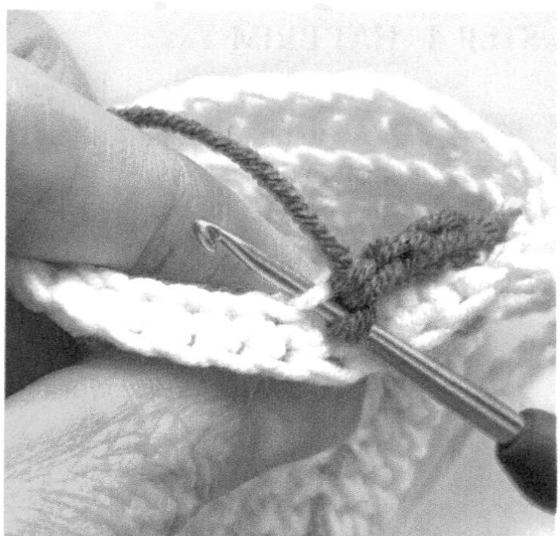

STEP 4 HAT BRIM

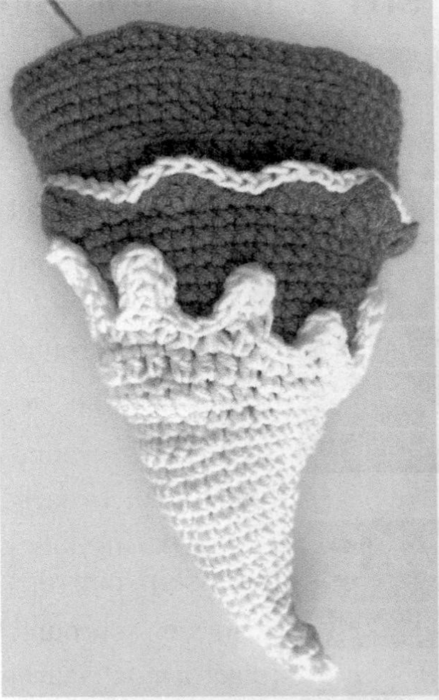

Grab the **Brown** yarn left on STEP 2 and continue crocheting:

Rd 25 *(SC in next 7sts, INC in next st, SC in next 7sts) from*rep x4 [64]

Rd 26 SC in each st around [64]

Rd 27 *(skip next st, 5DC in next st, skip next st, SC in next st) from*rep x16 [96]

Cut off Brown

Rd 28 **Join new Off-White** work loosely: slip stitch BLO in each st around.

Cut off Off-White

STEP 5 ICING SCALLOPS - 1ST LAYER

Rd 1 Hold the item upside down. Join **Brown** to stitch FLO with a marker #1 of STEP 2 Rd 11 and wor FLO: *(4DC in next st, skip next st, SC in next st, sl st in next st, SC in next st, hdc in next st, 3DC in next, hdc in next st, SC in next st, skip next st) from*rep x4, 4DC in next st, skip next st, SC in next, sl st in next st. [9 scallops]

Cut off Brown

Rd 2 With **Off-White**, work loosely: sl st BLO in each st around

Cut off Off-White

STEP 6 ICING SCALLOPS – 2nd LAYER

Rd 1 Hold the item upside down. Join **Brown** to stitch FLO with a marker #2 STEP 2 Rd 15 and work FLO: *(SC in next st, hdc in next st, 3DC in next, hdc in next st, SC in next st, skip next st, 4DC in next st, skip next st, SC in next st, sl st in next st)from*rep x5 [10 scallops]

Cut off Brown

Rd 2 With **Off-White**, work loosely: sl st BLO in each st around

Cut off Off-White

STEP 7 ICING SCALLOPS – 3rd LAYER

Rd 1 Hold the item upside down. Join **Brown** to stitch FLO with a marker #3 STEP 2 Rd 19 and work FLO: *(4DC in next st, skip next st, SC in next st, sl st in next st, SC in next st, hdc in next st, 3DC in next, hdc in next st, SC in next st, skip next st) from*rep x5, 4DC in next st, skip next st, SC in next st, sl st in next st [11 scallops]

Cut off Brown

Rd 2 With **Off-White**, work loosely: sl st BLO in each st around.

Cut off Off-White

STEP 8 BODY

Rd 1	**Honey caramel**. Work into stitches BLO of Rd 23 of STEP 2: SC BLO in each st around [60]
Rd 2	SC BLO in each st around [60]
Rd 3-4	SC in each st around [60]
Rd 5	*(SC in next 14sts, INC in next st)from*rep x4 [64]
Rd 6-12	SC in each st around [64]Change to Brown in last st
	Cut off Honey caramel
Rd 13	**Brown**: *(SC BLO in next 3sts, SC2tog BLO, SC BLO in next 3sts)from*rep x8 [56]
Rd 14	SC in each st around [56]
	Drop Brown yarn and make surface slip stitches in between Rd 12 and 13 around with **Off-white** yarn [56]
	Cut off Off-white
Rd 15	Grab **Brown** and continue working: *(SC in next 5sts, SC2tog)from*rep x8 [48]
Rd 16	SC in each st around [48]
Rd 17	SC BLO in each st around [48]
Rd 18	*(SC in next 2sts, SC2tog, SC in next 2sts)from*rep x8 [40]
Rd 19	*(SC in next 3sts, SC2tog)from*rep x8 [32]
Rd 20	*(SC in next st, SC2tog, SC in next st)from*rep x8 [24]
Rd 21	*(SC in next st, SC2tog)from*rep x8 [16]
	Stuff
Rd 22	SC2tog x8 [8]
	Cut off thread and sew the opening

STEP 9 STAND

Rd 1	With a new **Off-white** yarn work into stitches FLO of Rd 16 of the body: Ch1, SC FLO in each st around [48]
	Cut off thread

NOSE

Rd 1	**Wheat**: 6SC in magic ring, tighten the ring [6]
Rd 2	INC in each st around [12]
Rd 3	*(SC in next st, INC in next st)from*rep x6 [18]
Rd 4-5	SC in each st around [18]
Rd 6	*(SC in next st, SC2tog)from*rep x6 [12]
	Cut off thread leaving a long tail for sewing
	Stuff the nose a bit

BEARD

Rd 1	**White**: 6SC in magic ring, tighten the ring [6]
Rd 2	SC in each st around [6]
Rd 3	INC in each of next 6sts [12]
Rd 4	SC in next 2sts, 2hdc in each of next 2sts, SC in next 4sts, 2hdc in each of next 2sts, SC in next 2sts [16]
Rd 5	SC in next 3sts, 2hdc in each of next 2sts, SC in next 6sts, 2hdc in each of next 2sts, SC in next 3sts [20]
Rd 6	SC in next 4sts, 2hdc in each of next 2sts, SC in next 8sts, 2hdc in each of next 2sts, SC in next 4sts [24]
Rd 7	SC in next 5sts, 2hdc in each of next 2sts, SC in next 10sts, 2hdc in each of next 2sts, SC in next 5sts [28]
Rd 8	SC in next 6sts, 2hdc in each of next 2sts, SC in next 12sts, 2hdc in each of next 2sts, SC in next 6sts [32]
Rd 9-11	SC in each st around [32]
Rd 12	SC in next 6sts, SC2tog x2, SC in next 12sts, SC2tog x2, SC in next 6sts [28]
Rd 13	SC in next 5sts, SC2tog x2, SC in next 10sts, SC2tog x2, SC in next 5sts [24]
Rd 14	SC in next 4sts, SC2tog x2, SC in next 8sts, SC2tog x2, SC in next 4sts [20]
Rd 15	SC in next 3sts, SC2tog x2, SC in next 6sts, SC2tog x2, SC in next 3sts [16]
	Cut off thread leaving a long tail for sewing
	Sew or glue the nose on the beard and attach it all together under the hat brim in front.

ARMs

STEP 1 ARMS

Rd 1	**Wheat**: 5SC in magic ring, tighten the ring [5]
Rd 2	INC in each st around [10]
Rd 3-5	SC in each st around [10] Change to Honey Caramel in last st
	Cut off Wheat
Rd 6-7	**Honey caramel**: SC in each st around [10]
Rd 8	SC BLO in each st around [10]
Rd 9-17	SC in each st around [10]
	Cut off yarn leaving a long tail for sewing

STEP 2 CUFF

Rd 1	**Off-white** work into stitches FLO of Rd 7: DC FLO in each st around [10]
	Cut off thread
	Sew the arms to the body under the hat brim.

Sew or glue beads on the gnome's hat.

Sew or glue the drips to the brown part to give it a neat look.

Christmas Gnome with stripes

SIZE: 26 cm / 10 in

	COLOR AND YARN	TOTAL FOR A PROJECT
Honey caramel	Yarn Art Jeans 07	Approx. 18g/60meters
Off-white	Yarn Art Jeans 03	Approx. 5g/20meters
Wheat	Yarn Art Jeans 05	Approx. 7g/25meters
Brown	Yarn Art Jeans 40	Approx. 22g/70metetrs
White	Yarn Art Jeans 62	Approx. 7g/25meters
FOR FLOWERS (flower pattern on page 14)		
Red	Yarn Art Jeans 90	Approx. 5g/20meters
Light Green	Yarn Art Jeans 82	Approx. 5g/20meters

OTHER MATERIALS

- Stuffing approx. 50g

CROCHET STICHES:

Ch, SC, hdc, INC, sl st, SC2tog, FLO, BLO

NOTE: When change a yarn cut off if it's stated in a pattern in other cases, drop a yarn and raise when it's needed. Use a contrast thread to mark the beginning of each round. Do not remove it until your work is completed.

STEP 1 HAT

Rd 1	**Honey caramel**: 6SC in magic ring, tighten the ring [6]
Rd 2	SC in each st around [6]
Rd 3	*(SC in next st, INC in next st)from*rep x3 [9]
Rd 4	SC in each st around [9]
Rd 5	*(SC in next st, INC in next st, SC in next st) from*rep x3 [12]
Rd 6	SC in each st around [12]
Rd 7	*(SC in next st, INC in next st, SC in next st) from*rep x4 [16]
Rd 8-9	SC in each st around [16]
Rd 10	*(SC in next 3sts, INC in next st)from*rep x4 [20]
Rd 11-12	SC in each st around [20] Change to Brown in last st

NOTE: This technique can make a color change less visible: To change the color, you can crochet Slip Stitch(instead of 1st SC) as the first stitch of each round where you change a color.

Rd 13	**Brown**: *(SC in next 2sts, INC in next st, SC in next 2sts) from*rep x4 [24]
Rd 14-15	SC in each st around.[24] Change to Off-white in last st
Rd 16	**Off-white**: *(SC in next 5sts, INC in next st)from*rep x4 [28]
Rd 17-18	SC in each st around [28] Change to Honey Caramel in last st
Rd 19	**Honey caramel**: *(SC in next 3sts, INC in next st, SC in next 3sts)from*rep x4 [32]
Rd 20-21	SC in each st around [32] Chanhe to Brown in last st
Rd 22	**Brown**: *(SC in next 7sts, INC in next st) from*rep x4 [36]
Rd 23-24	SC in each st around [36]Change to Off-White in last st
Rd 25	**Off-white**: *(SC in next 4sts, INC in next st, SC in next 4sts) from*rep x4 [40]
Rd 26-27	SC in each st around [40]Change to Honey Caramel in last st
Rd 28	**Honey caramel**: *(SC in next 9sts, INC in next st) from*rep x4 [44]
Rd 29-30	SC in each st around[44] Change to Brown in last st

Rd 31	**Brown**: *(SC in next 5sts, INC in next st, SC in next 5sts) from*rep x4 [48]
Rd 32-33	SC in each st around[48] Change to Off-white in last st
	Cut off Brown
Rd 34	**Off-white**: *(SC in next 11sts, INC in next st) from*rep x4 [52]
Rd 35-36	SC in each st around [52] Chage to Honey Caramel in last st
	Cut off Off-white
Rd 37	**Honey caramel**: *(SC in next 6sts, INC in next st, SC in next 6sts) from*rep x4 [56]
Rd 38-39	SC in each st around [56]
Rd 40-41	SC BLO in each st around[56] Change to Brown in last st
	Cut off Honey caramel
Rd 42-45	**Brown**: SC in each st around [56]
Rd 46	*(SC in next 13sts, INC in next st)from*rep x4 [60]
Rd 47-50	SC in each st around [60]
Rd 51	*(SC in next 7sts, INC in next st, SC in next 7sts) from*rep x4 [64]
Rd 52-53	SC in each st around [64]
Rd 54	*(SC in next 3sts, SC2tog, SC in next 3sts) from*rep x8 [56]
Rd 55-57	SC in each st around[56] Stuff the hat
Rd 58	*(SC in next 5sts, SC2tog)from*rep x8 [48]
Rd 59-60	SC in each st around [48]
Rd 61	SC BLO in each st around [48]
Rd 62	*(SC in next 2sts, SC2tog, SC in next 2sts) from*rep x8 [40]
	Stuff the body
Rd 63	*(SC in next 3sts, SC2tog)from*rep x8 [32]
Rd 64	*(SC in next st, SC2tog, SC in next st)from*rep x8 [24]
Rd 65	*(SC in next st, SC2tog)from*rep x8 [16]
	Stuff the body
Rd 66	SC2tog x8 [8]
	Cut off thread and sew the opening

STEP 2 HAT BRIM

Rd 1	With **Honey caramel** start from 39th rd of the hat: *(SC FLO in next 13sts, INC FLO in next st) from*rep x4 [60]
Rd 2	*(hdc in next 9sts, INC in next st)from*rep x6 [66]
Rd 3	*(hdc in next 5sts, INC in next st, hdc in next 5sts) from rep x6 [72]

Rd 4-6	hdc in each st around [72]
Rd 7	sl st in each st around [72]
	Cut off thread

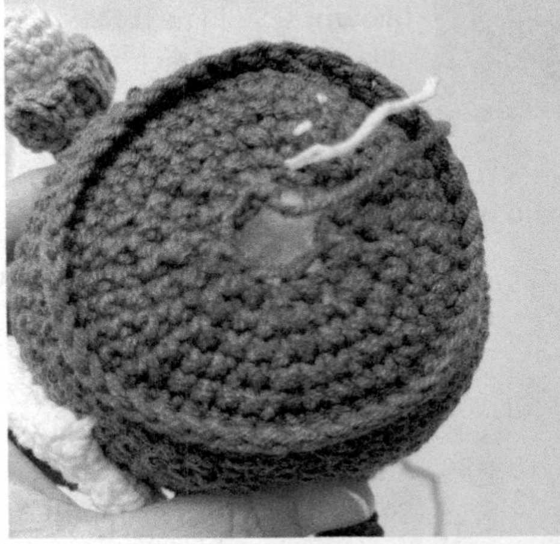

STEP 3 STAND

With a new **Brown** work into available loops of stitches of Rd 60 of the body: Ch1, SC FLO in each st around [48]

Cut off thread

BEARD

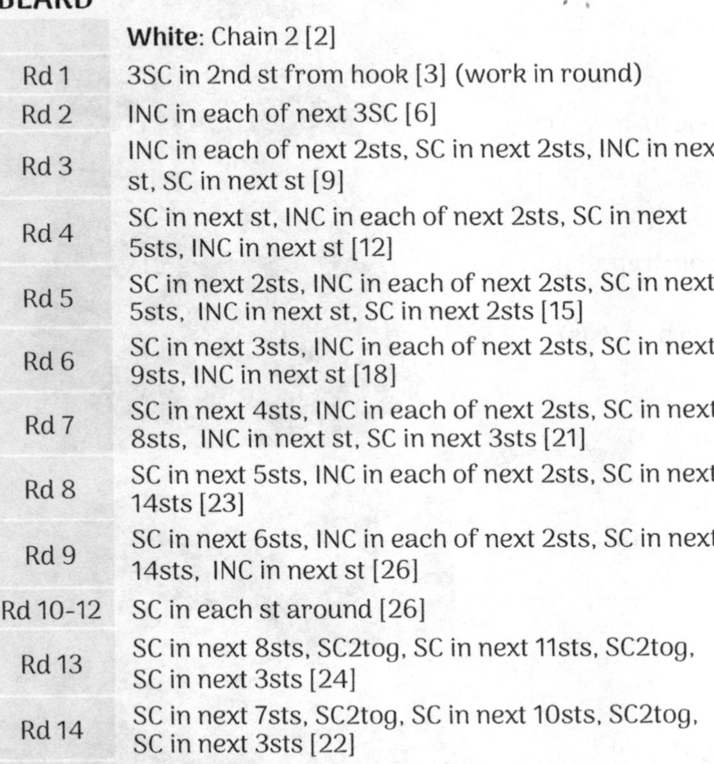

	White: Chain 2 [2]
Rd 1	3SC in 2nd st from hook [3] (work in round)
Rd 2	INC in each of next 3SC [6]
Rd 3	INC in each of next 2sts, SC in next 2sts, INC in next st, SC in next st [9]
Rd 4	SC in next st, INC in each of next 2sts, SC in next 5sts, INC in next st [12]
Rd 5	SC in next 2sts, INC in each of next 2sts, SC in next 5sts, INC in next st, SC in next 2sts [15]
Rd 6	SC in next 3sts, INC in each of next 2sts, SC in next 9sts, INC in next st [18]
Rd 7	SC in next 4sts, INC in each of next 2sts, SC in next 8sts, INC in next st, SC in next 3sts [21]
Rd 8	SC in next 5sts, INC in each of next 2sts, SC in next 14sts [23]
Rd 9	SC in next 6sts, INC in each of next 2sts, SC in next 14sts, INC in next st [26]
Rd 10-12	SC in each st around [26]
Rd 13	SC in next 8sts, SC2tog, SC in next 11sts, SC2tog, SC in next 3sts [24]
Rd 14	SC in next 7sts, SC2tog, SC in next 10sts, SC2tog, SC in next 3sts [22]
Rd 15	SC in next 6sts, SC2tog, SC in next 9sts, SC2tog, SC in next 3sts [20]
	Cut off thread leaving a long tail for sewing

NOSE

Rd 1	**Wheat**: 6SC in magic ring, tighten the ring [6]
Rd 2	INC in each st around [12]
Rd 3	*(SC in next st, INC in next st)from*rep x6 [18]
Rd 4-5	SC in each st around [18]
Rd 6	*(SC in next st, SC2tog)from*rep x6 [12]
	Cut off thread leaving a long tail for sewing. Stuff the nose a bit. Sew or glue the nose on the beard

ARMs

STEP 1 PALMS

Rd 1	**Wheat**: 5SC in magic ring, tighten the ring [5]
Rd 2	INC in each of next 5sts [10]
Rd 3	SC in each st around [10]
Rd 4	SC in next 4sts, SC FLO in next st, Ch2, SC in 2nd Ch (to shape a thumb), SC in next 5 sts [13]
Rd 5	SC in next 4sts, SC BLO in next st, skip 3 stitches of a thumb, SC in next 5sts [10] Change to Off-white in last st.
	Cut off Wheat
Rd 6-7	**Off-white**: SC in each st around [10] Change to Brown in last st. Cut off Off-white
Rd 8	**Brown**: SC BLO in each st around [10]
Rd 9-17	SC in each st around [10]
	Cut off thread leaving a long tail for sewing

STEP 2 CUFF

Rd 1	With a new **Honey caramel** work into 7th rd: hdc FLO in each st around [10]
Rd 2	hdc in next 10sts, sl st in next st [10]
	Cut off thread

Sew the beard with the nose to the body in front under the hat brim. Sew the arms to the body.

Idea: You can make flowers and decorate the hat as it's illustrated in the image. Flower pattern: see page 14

Xmas Flower Stripes

SIZE: 26 cm / 10 in

Use different colors, different stripe heights and stripes amount, decorative elements, and create your own unique gnomes.

Decorate the hat with Christmas Flowers to add a Christmas vibe.

Flower Patterns – see page 14.

Santa

SIZE: 23 cm / 9 in

	COLOR AND YARN	TOTAL FOR A PROJECT
Red	★ Yarn Art Jeans 90	Approx.30g/105 meters
White	Yarn Art Jeans 62	Approx.15g/50 meters
Wheat	★ Yarn Art Jeans 05	Approx.7g/20 meters
White Fur (fleece style yarn)	☆ Some yarn ideas: Scheepjes Softy Rico Baby Teddy Aran White Sirdar Snuggly Snowflake Chunky Milky or any similar yarn	Approx.15g/50meters
Black	★ Yarn Art Jeans 53	Approx.12g/40 meters
Yellow	★ Yarn Art Jeans 58	Approx. 3g

OTHER MATERIALS

- Stuffing approx. 50g

CROCHET STICHES:

Ch, SC, hdc, DC, INC, sl st, SC2tog, FLO, BLO
Surface slip stitch

Use a contrast thread to mark the beginning of each round.
Do not remove it until your work is completed.

STEP 1 HAT

Rd 1	**Red**: 6SC in magic ring, tighten the ring [6]
Rd 2	SC in each st around [6]
Rd 3	*(SC in next st, INC in next st)from*rep x3 [9]
Rd 4	SC in each st around [9]
Rd 5	*(SC in next st, INC in next st, SC in next st) from*rep x3 [12]
Rd 6	SC in each st around [12]
Rd 7	SC in next 4sts, INC in each of next 4sts, SC in next 4sts [16]
Rd 8-9	SC in each st around [16]
Rd 10	SC in next 6sts, INC in each of next 4sts, SC in next 6sts [20]
Rd 11	SC in next 8sts, INC in each of next 4sts, SC in next 8sts [24]
Rd 12-13	SC in next st, SC2tog, SC in next 8sts, INC in each of next 2sts, SC in next 8sts, SC2tog, SC in next st [24]
Rd 14	*(SC in next 5sts, INC in next st)from*rep x4 [28]
Rd 15	SC in each st around [28]
Rd 16	SC in next 2sts, SC2tog, SC in next 9sts, INC in each of next 2sts, SC in next 9sts, SC2tog, SC in next 2sts [28]
Rd 17	SC in each st around [28]
Rd 18	SC in next 2sts, SC2tog, SC in next 9sts, INC in each of next 2sts, SC in next 9sts, SC2tog, SC in next 2sts [28]
Rd 19	*(SC in next 3sts, INC in next st, SC in next 3sts) from*rep x4 [32]
Rd 20	SC in each st around [32]
Rd 21	SC in next st, SC2tog, SC in next 12sts, INC in each of next 2sts, SC in next 12sts, SC2tog, SC in next st [32]
Rd 22	*(SC in next 7sts, INC in next st)from*rep x4 [36]
Rd 23	SC in each st around [36]
Rd 24	SC in next 2sts, SC2tog, SC in next 13sts, INC in each of next 2sts, SC in next 13sts, SC2tog, SC in next 2sts [36]
Rd 25	*(SC in next 4sts, INC in next st, SC in next 4sts) from*rep x4 [40]
Rd 26	SC in each st around [40]
Rd 27	SC in next 2sts, SC2tog, SC in next 15sts, INC in each of next 2sts, SC in next 15sts, SC2tog, SC in next 2sts [40]
Rd 28	*(SC in next 9sts, INC in next st)from*rep x4 [44]
Rd 29-30	SC in each st around [44]
Rd 31	*(SC in next 5sts, INC in next st, SC in next 5sts) from*rep x4 [48]
Rd 32-33	SC in each st around [48]

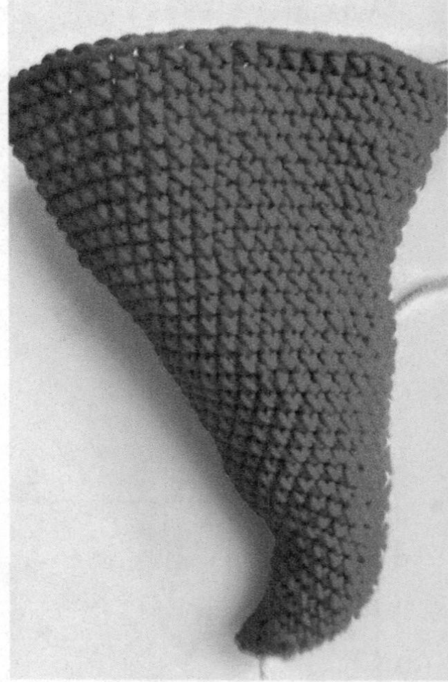

Rd 34	*(SC in next 11sts, INC in next st)from*rep x4 [52]
Rd 35-36	SC in each st around [52]
Rd 37	*(SC in next 6sts, INC in next st, SC in next 6sts)from*rep x4 [56]
Rd 38-39	SC in each st around [56]
Rd 40-41	SC BLO in each st around [56] From 41 to Rd 51 change color in last st in every round. Cut off thread when it's stated

STEP 2 CONTINUE — BODY

Rd 42	**White**: SC in each st around [56]
Rd 43	**Red**: SC in each st around [56]
Rd 44	**White**: SC in each st around [56]
Rd 45	**Red**: SC in each st around [56]
Rd 46	**White**: *(SC in next 13sts, INC in next st) from*rep x4 [60]
Rd 47	**Red**: SC in each st around [60]
Rd 48	**White**: SC in each st around [60]
Rd 49	**Red**: SC in each st around [60]
Rd 50	**White**: SC in next 59sts, sl st in next st [60] Change to Red in last st
	Cut off White
Rd 51	**Red**: *(SC in next 7sts, INC in next st, SC in next 7sts) from*rep x4 [64]
	Change to Black and leave Red on wrong side

STEP 3 CONTINUE — BELT

Rd 52	**Black**: SC BLO in each st around [64]
Rd 53	SC in each st around [64]
Rd 54	SC in each st around [64] Change to Red in last st(leave Black on a wrong side, we will use it to make Belt Decoration)

STEP 4 CONTINUE — PANTS

Rd 55	**Grab Red**: *(SC BLO in next 3sts, SC2tog BLO, SC BLO in next 3sts)from*rep x8 [56]
Rd 56-57	SC in each st around [56]
	Drop the loop and leave it for awhile
	Stuff

BELT DECORATION

Grab **Black**:
1) work surface slip stitch into each stitches of Rd 51 [64];
2) work surface slip stitch into each stitches of Rd 55 [56];
Cut off Black. Leave a tail on a wrong side

Continue working on the pants with Red yarn

Rd 58	*(SC in next 5sts, SC2tog)from*rep x8 [48]
Rd 59-60	SC in each st around [48]
Rd 61	SC BLO in each st around [48]
Rd 62	*(SC in next 2sts, SC2tog, SC in next 2sts) from*rep x8 [40]
	Stuff
Rd 63	*(SC in next 3sts, SC2tog)from*rep x8 [32]
Rd 64	*(SC in next st, SC2tog, SC in next st)from*rep x8 [24]
Rd 65	*(SC in next st, SC2tog)from*rep x8 [16]
	Stuff
Rd 66	SC2tog x8 Cut off thread and sew the opening [8]

STEP 5 HAT BRIM

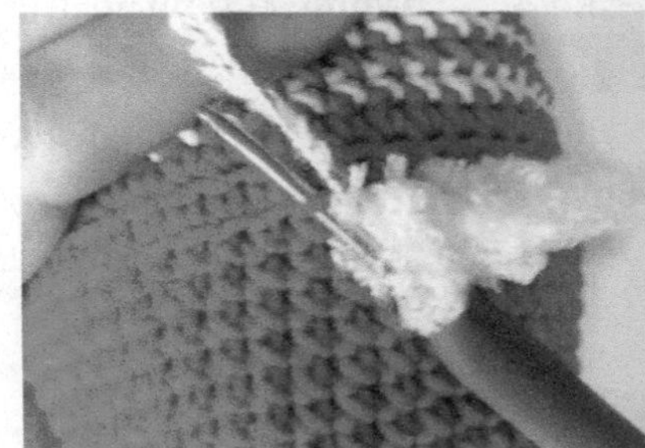

Rd 1	**White Fur**: work into stitches FLO of Rd 39 of the hat: *(DC FLO in next 8sts, 2DC FLO in next st) from*rep x6, DC FLO in next 2sts [62]
Rd 2	*(DC in next 9sts, 2DC in next st)from*rep x6, DC in next 2sts [68]
	Cut off thread

STEP 6 STAND

With **Red** work into stitches FLO of Rd 60 of the body: Ch1, SC FLO in each st around [48]

Cut off thread

STEP 7 FRAME BUCKLE

With **Yellow**: Embroider the frame buckle

Make a white pompon and sew or glue it to the hat

MUSTACHE make x2

Rd 1	**White**: 4SC in magic ring, tighten the ring [4]
Rd 2	*(SC in next st, INC in next st)from*rep x2 [6]
Rd 3	INC in each of next 2sts, SC in next 4sts [8]
Rd 4	SC in next st, INC in each of next 2sts, SC in next 5sts [10]
Rd 5-8	SC in each st around [10]
Rd 9	SC2tog x5 [5]

Cut off thread leaving a long tail for sewing. Sew or glue the nose and the mustache to the body in front under the hat brim as it's illustrated in image

NOSE

Rd 1	**Wheat**: 6SC in magic ring, tighten the ring [6]
Rd 2	INC in each st around [12]
Rd 3	*(SC in next st, INC in next st)from*rep x6 [18]
Rd 4-5	SC in each st around [18]
Rd 6	*(SC in next st, SC2tog)from*rep x6 [12]

Cut off thread leaving a long tail for sewing. Stuff the nose a bit

BOOTS

Rd 1	**Black**: 6SC in magic ring, tighten the ring [6]
Rd 2	INC each st around [12]
Rd 3	*(SC in next st, INC in next st)from*rep x6 [18]
Rd 4-6	SC in each st around [18]
Rd 7	*(SC in next st, SC2tog)from*rep x6 [12]
	Fold in half, stuff and stitch edges together by SC (SC in 6sts) Cut off thread leaving a long tail for sewing. Sew the boot to a stand's round on the body.
	Embroider a frame buckle with **Yellow**.

ARMs

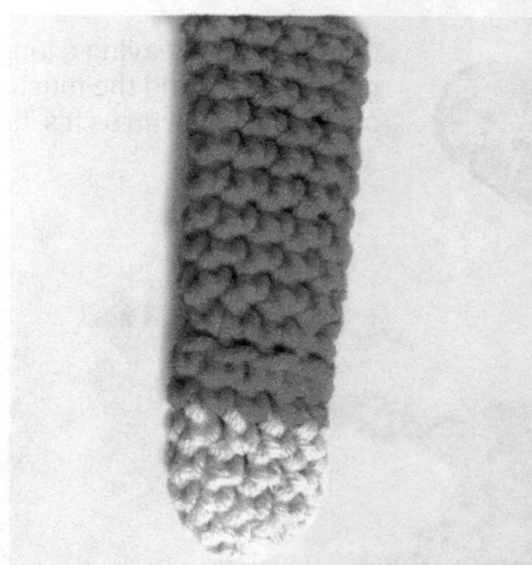

STEP 1 PALMS

Rd 1	**Wheat**: 5SC in magic ring, tighten the ring [5]
Rd 2	INC in each st around [10]
Rd 3-5	SC in each st around [10] Change to Red in last st
	Cut off Wheat
Rd 6-7	**Red**: SC in each st around [10]
Rd 8	SC BLO in each st around [10]
Rd 9-17	SC in each st around [10]
	Cut off thread leaving a long tail for sewing

STEP 2 CUFF

Rd 1	With a new **White Fur**: work into 7th rd: DC FLO in each st around [10]
	Cut off thread
	Wheat: embroider a thumb
	Sew the arms to the body under the hat brim.

Rudolph the Red-Nosed reindeer

SIZE: 23 cm / 9 in

	COLOR AND YARN	TOTAL FOR A PROJECT
Light brown	Yarn Art Jeans 71	Approx. 25g/80meters
Dark Brown	Yarn Art Jeans 70	Approx. 30g/100meters
Wheat	Yarn Art Jeans 05	Approx. 5g/20meters
White	Yarn Art Jeans 62	Approx. 10g/35meters
Red	Yarn Art Jeans 90	Approx. 5g/20meters

OTHER MATERIALS

- Stuffing approx. 50g

CROCHET STICHES:

Ch, SC, INC, sl st, SC2tog, FLO, BLO

Use a contrast thread to mark the beginning of each round.
Do not remove it until your work is completed.

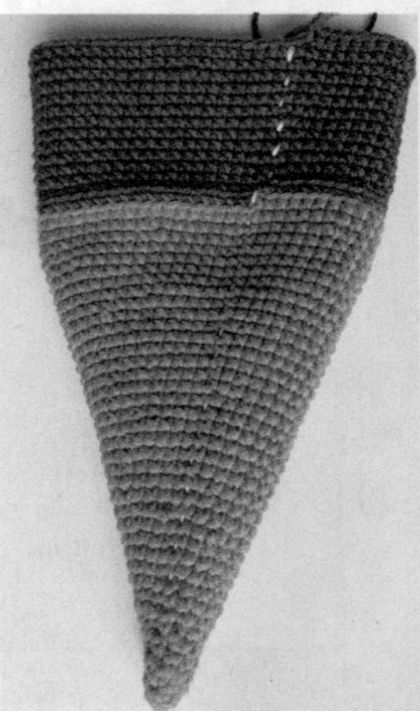

STEP 1 HAT

Rd 1	**Light brown**: 6SC in magic ring, tighten the ring [6]
Rd 2	SC in each st around [6]
Rd 3	*(SC in next st, INC in next st)from*rep x3 [9]
Rd 4	SC in each st around [9]
Rd 5	*(SC in next st, INC in next st, SC in next st)from*rep x3 [12]
Rd 6	SC in each st around [12]
Rd 7	*(SC in next st, INC in next st, SC in next st)from*rep x4 [16]
Rd 8-9	SC in each st around [16]
Rd 10	*(SC in next 3sts, INC in next st)from*rep x4 [20]
Rd 11-12	SC in each st around [20]
Rd 13	*(SC in next 2sts, INC in next st, SC in next 2sts) from*rep x4 [24]
Rd 14-15	SC in each st around [24]
Rd 16	*(SC in next 5sts, INC in next st)from*rep x4 [28]
Rd 17-18	SC in each st around [28]
Rd 19	*(SC in next 3sts, INC in next st, SC in next 3sts) from*rep x4 [32]
Rd 20-21	SC in each st around [32]
Rd 22	*(SC in next 7sts, INC in next st)from*rep x4 [36]
Rd 23-24	SC in each st around [36]
Rd 25	*(SC in next 4sts, INC in next st, SC in next 4sts) from*rep x4 [40]
Rd 26-27	SC in each st around [40]
Rd 28	*(SC in next 9sts, INC in next st)from*rep x4 [44]
Rd 29-30	SC in each st around [44]
Rd 31	*(SC in next 5sts, INC in next st, SC in next 5sts) from*rep x4 [48]
Rd 32-33	SC in each st around [48]
Rd 34	*(SC in next 11sts, INC in next st)from*rep x4 [52]
Rd 35-36	SC in each st around [52]
Rd 37	*(SC in next 6sts, INC in next st, SC in next 6sts) from*rep x4 [56]
Rd 38	SC in each st around[56]Change to Dark Brown in last st. Cut off Light Brown
Rd 39-40	**Dark Brown**: SC BLO in each st around [56]
Rd 41-45	SC in each st around [56]
Rd 46	*(SC in next 13sts, INC in next st)from*rep x4 [60]
Rd 47-50	SC in each st around [60]
Rd 51	*(SC in next 7sts, INC in next st, SC in next 7sts) from*rep x4 [64]
Rd 52-53	SC in each st around [64]

Rd 54	*(SC in next 3sts, SC2tog, SC in next 3sts)from*rep x8 [56]
Rd 55-57	SC in each st around [56]
	Stuff
Rd 58	*(SC in next 5sts, SC2tog)from*rep x8 [48]
Rd 59-60	SC in each st around [48]
Rd 61	SC BLO in each st around [48]
Rd 62	*(SC in next 2sts, SC2tog, SC in next 2sts)from*rep x8 [40]
	Stuff
Rd 63	*(SC in next 3sts, SC2tog)from*rep x8 [32]
Rd 64	*(SC in next st, SC2tog, SC in next st)from*rep x8 [24]
Rd 65	*(SC in next st, SC2tog)from*rep x8 [16]
	Stuff
Rd 66	SC2tog x8 [8]
	Cut off thread and sew the opening

STEP 2 STAND

Rd 1	With **Dark Brown** work into stitches FLO of Rd 60 of the body: Ch1, SC FLO in each st around [48]
	Cut off thread

STEP 3 HAT BRIM

	Light brown: Chain 10 [10]
Row 1	SC in 2nd st from hook, SC in next 8sts [9]
Row 2-58	Ch1, SC BLO in each st around [9]
	Fold the detail in half and stitch short edges together by SC [9]
	Cut off thread

BEARD

Rd 1	**White**: 6SC in magic ring, tighten the ring [6]
Rd 2	SC in each st around [6]
Rd 3	INC in each each st around [12]
Rd 4	SC in next 2sts, INC in each of next 2sts, SC in next 4sts, INC in each of next 2sts, SC in next 2sts [16]
Rd 5	SC in next 3sts, INC in each of next 2sts, SC in next 6sts, INC in each of next 2sts, SC in next 3sts [20]
Rd 6	SC in next 4sts, INC in each of next 2sts, SC in next 8sts, INC in each of next 2sts, SC in next 4sts [24]
Rd 7	SC in next 5sts, INC in each of next 2sts, SC in next 10sts, INC in each of next 2sts, SC in next 5sts [28]
Rd 8	SC in next 6sts, INC in each of next 2sts, SC in next 12sts, INC in each of next 2sts, SC in next 6sts [32]

Rd 9-11	SC in each st around [32]
Rd 12	SC in next 6sts, SC2tog x2, SC in next 12sts, SC2tog x2, SC in next 6sts [28]
Rd 13	SC in next 5sts, SC2tog x2, SC in next 10sts, SC2tog x2, SC in next 5sts [24]
Rd 14	SC in next 4sts, SC2tog x2, SC in next 8sts, SC2tog x2, SC in next 4sts [20]
Rd 15	SC in next 3sts, SC2tog x2, SC in next 6sts, SC2tog x2, SC in next 3sts [16]
	Cut off thread leaving a long tail for sewing

ARMs

STEP 1 ARM

Rd 1	**Wheat**: 5SC in magic ring, tighten the ring [5]
Rd 2	INC in each st around [10]
Rd 3-5	SC in each st around [10] Change to Dark Brown in last st
	Cut off Wheat
Rd 6-17	**Dark Brown**: SC in each st around [10]
	Cut off thread leaving a long tail for sewing

STEP 2 CUFF

	Light brown Foundation chain: Chain 4 [4]
Row 1	SC in 2nd st from hook, SC in next 2sts [3]
Row 2-11	Ch1, SC BLO in each st around [3]
	Stitch short edges together by SC Attach the cuff to the arm

NOSE

Rd 1	**Red**: 6SC in magic ring, tighten the ring [6]
Rd 2	INC in each st around [12]
Rd 3	*(SC in next st, INC in next st)from*rep x6 [18]
Rd 4-5	SC in each st around [18]
Rd 6	*(SC in next st, SC2tog)from*rep x6 [12]
	Cut off thread leaving a long tail for sewing Stuff the nose a bit

ANTLERS x2. Dark Brown

STEP 1 SMALL BRANCH x1

Rd 1 6SC in magic ring, tighten the ring. Tighten the ring [6]

Rd 2 *(SC in next st, 2SC in next st) from*rep x3 [9]

Rd 3-5 SC in each stitch around [9]

Cut off a thread

STEP 2 LARGE BRANCHES OF THE ANTLER x2

Repeat Rd 1-5 as for the small branch and continue working SC in each stitch around up to 7 rounds. Cut off yarn, for the second large branch don't cut off a thread and go to STEP 3 – ASSEMBLE

STEP 3 ASSEMBLE. VIDEO: How to join antlers

Join 2 large antlers(pic.1) together by SC in 4 stitches inserting your hook through both fabrics (pic.2)

Rd 1 Work around the edge: SC in 5sts of the 1st antler (pic.2 – yellow arrow), then work into edge stitches of the 2nd antler: SC in 5sts (pic.2 – green arrow)

Rd 2 SC in each of 10sts stitches around both antlers
SC in next st, join the small antler by SC in 4 stitches inserting your hook through both fabrics as we did it when joining the large antlers together

Rd 3 Work around the edge of both antlers: SC in next 6sts of the large antler, SC in next 5sts of the small antler

Rd 4-6 SC in each of 11 stitches around

Stuff as you work. Cut off a thread leaving a long tail for sewing.

Scan for the video tutorial

Attach the arms. The nose and the beard to the body as is it illustrated in the image.

Attach the brim to the body above the nose covering the arm seams. And then attach the antlers.

WE WISH YOU
Merry
CHRISTMAS
and
Happy new year

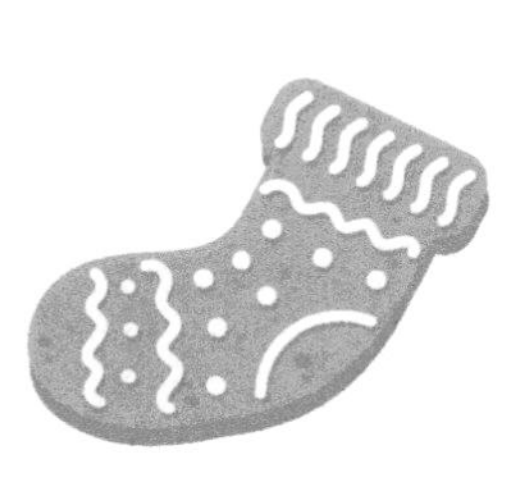

SIZE: 17 cm / 7 in

	COLOR AND YARN	TOTAL FOR A PROJECT
Honey caramel	Yarn Art Jeans 07	Approx. 15g/55meters
Dark Brown	Yarn Art Jeans 70	Approx. 10g/35meters
Off-white	Yarn Art Jeans 03	Approx. 15g/55meters
White	Yarn Art Jeans 62	Approx. 5g/15meters
Red	Yarn Art Jeans 90	Approx. 15g/55meters
Bright Green	Yarn Art Jeans 52	Approx. 2g
Wheat	Yarn Art Jeans 05	Approx. 5g/15meters

OTHER MATERIALS

- Stuffing approx. 50g
- Chenille-covered wire approx.15cm

CROCHET STICHES:

Ch, SC, hdc, INC, sl st, SC2tog, FLO, BLO

Use a contrast thread to mark the beginning of each round.
Do not remove it until your work is completed.

STEP 1 HAT

Rd 1	**Dark Brown**: 6SC in magic ring, tighten the ring [6]
Rd 2	INC in each of next 6sts [12]
Rd 3	*(SC in next st, INC in next st)from*rep x6 [18]
Rd 4	*(SC in next st, INC in next st, SC in next st) from*rep x6 [24]
Rd 5	*(SC in next 3sts, INC in next st)from*rep x6 [30]
Rd 6	*(SC in next 2sts, INC in next st, SC in next 2sts) from*rep x6 [36]
	Check gauge/tension: Ø4.5-5cm
Rd 7	*(SC in next 5sts, INC in next st)from*rep x6 [42]
Rd 8	*(SC in next 3sts, INC in next st, SC in next 3sts) from*rep x6 [48]
Rd 9	*(SC in next 7sts, INC in next st)from*rep x6 [54]
Rd 10	*(SC in next 4sts, INC in next st, SC in next 4sts) from*rep x6 [60]
Rd 11-19	SC in each st around [60] Change to Honey Caramel in last st
	Cut off Dark Brown

STEP 2 CONTINUE - BODY

Rd 20-21	**Honey caramel**: SC BLO in each st around [60]
Rd 22-36	SC in each st around [60]
Rd 37	*(SC in next 13sts, SC2tog)from*rep x4 [56]
Rd 38	*(SC in next 6sts, SC2tog, SC in next 6sts) from*rep x4 [52]
Rd 39	*(SC in next 11sts, SC2tog)from*rep x4 [48]
Rd 40	SC BLO in each st around [48]
Rd 41	*(SC in next 2sts, SC2tog, SC in next 2sts) from*rep x8 [40]
	Stuff
Rd 42	*(SC in next 3sts, SC2tog)from*rep x8 [32]
Rd 43	*(SC in next st, SC2tog, SC in next st) from*rep x8 [24]
Rd 44	*(SC in next st, SC2tog)from*rep x8 [16]
	Stuff
Rd 45	SC2tog x8 [8]
	Cut off thread leaving a long tail and sew the opening

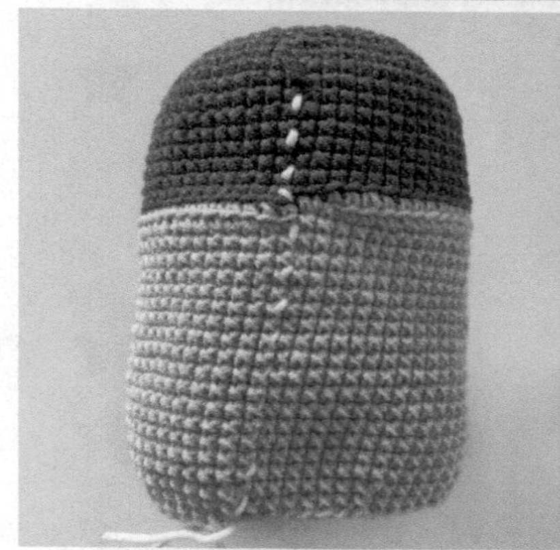

STEP 3 BOTTOM DECORATION — CREAM

Rd 1	**Off-white**: work into stitches of Rd 39: INC FLO in each st around
Rd 2	*(SC in next st, INC in next st)from*rep to end
	Cut off thread

DECORATION: CREAM TOPPING

Rd 1-9	**Off-white**: Repeat STEP 1 Rd 1-9
	Continue: make drips:
	The first drip is based on a foundation chain 5:
	Chain 5 (pic.1), hdc in 2nd Ch from hook (pic.2), hdc in each st of chain (pic.3), hdc in stitch of main part where Ch5 comes from (pic.4), skip next st of a main part, SC in next 4sts of main part (pic.5)

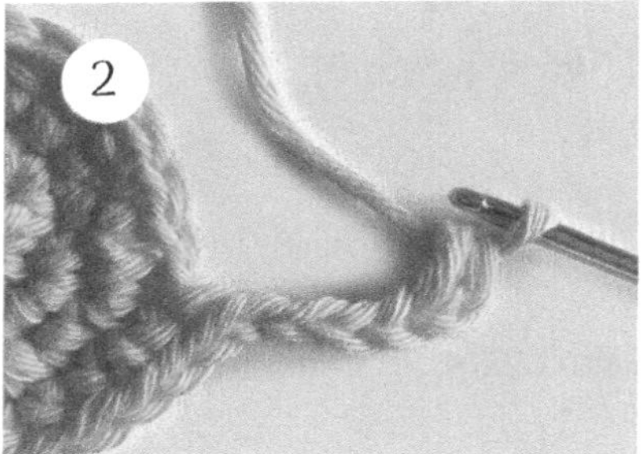

The same way we make drips based on different foundation chain lengths and make different number of SC between drips to separate them, for example, I did:

Ch5-4SC between-Ch5-3SC between-Ch3-3SC between-Ch5-4SC between-Ch2-3SC between-Ch5-2SC between-Ch6-4SC between-Ch7-3SC between-Ch4-4SC between-Ch4-4SC between-Ch7-3SC between- Ch3 – slip stitch

Cut off thread

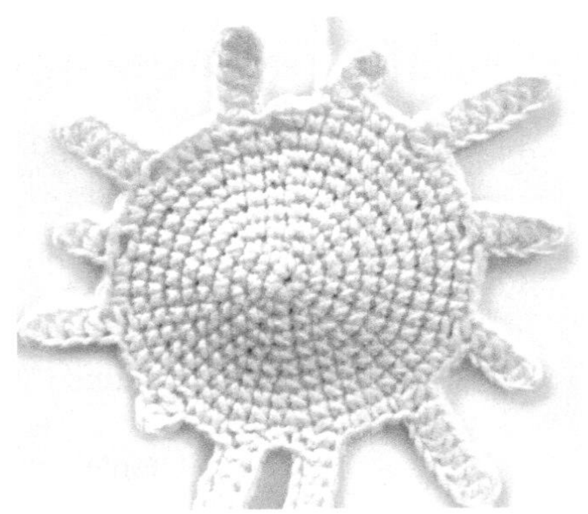

NOSE

Rd 1	**Wheat**: 6SC in magic ring, tighten the ring [6]
Rd 2	INC in each st around [12]
Rd 3	*(SC in next st, INC in next st)from*rep x6 [18]
Rd 4-5	SC in each st around [18]
Rd 6	*(SC in next st, SC2tog)from*rep x6 [12]

Cut off thread leaving a long tail for sewing.

Stuff the nose a bit. Sew or glue the nose to the beard

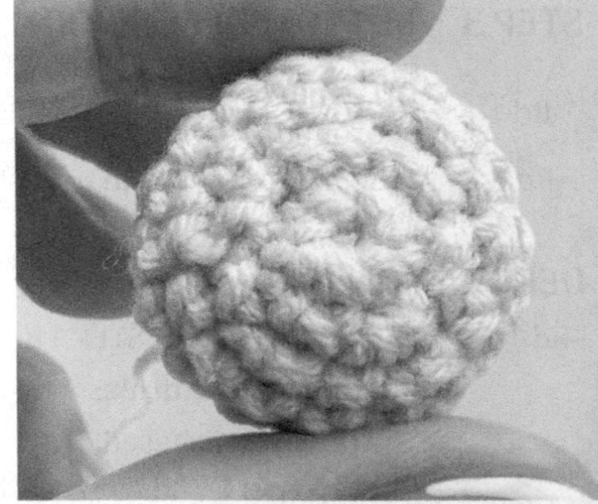

BEARD

	White: Chain 2 [2]
Rd 1	3SC in 2nd st from hook [3] (work in round)
Rd 2	INC in each of next 3sts [6]
Rd 3	INC in each of next 2sts, SC in next 2sts, INC in next st, SC in next st [9]
Rd 4	SC in next st, INC in each of next 2sts, SC in next 5sts, INC in next st [12]
Rd 5	SC in next 2sts, INC in each of next 2sts, SC in next 5sts, INC in next st, SC in next 2sts [15]
Rd 6	SC in next 3sts, INC in each of next 2sts, SC in next 9sts, INC in next st [18]
Rd 7	SC in next 4sts, INC in each of next 2sts, SC in next 8sts, INC in next st, SC in next 3sts [21]
Rd 8	SC in next 5sts, INC in each of next 2sts, SC in next 9sts, INC in next st, SC in next 4sts [24]
Rd 9-11	SC in each st around [24]
Rd 12	SC in next 7sts, SC2tog, SC in next 10sts, SC2tog, SC in next 3sts [22]
Rd 13	SC in next 6sts, SC2tog, SC in next 9sts, SC2tog, SC in next 3sts [20]
Rd 14	SC in each st around [20]

Cut of thread leaving a long tail for sewing

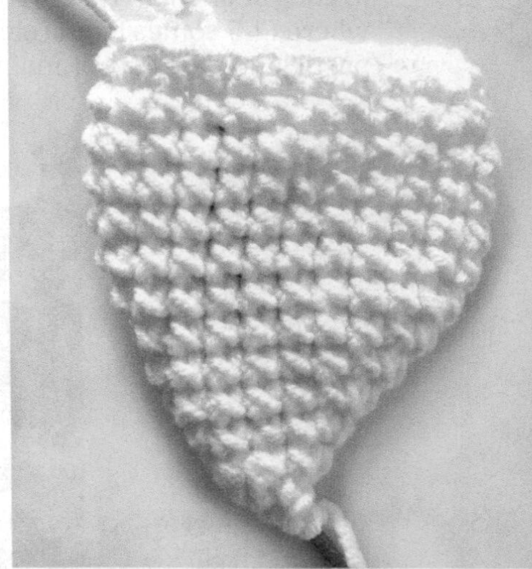

HAT BRIM

	Red Foundations chain: Chain 8 [8]
Row 1	SC in 2nd st from hook, SC in next 6sts [7] Ch1, Turn
Row 2-80	SC BLO in each st across [7]Ch1, Turn
Row 81	Continue working into long edge: [60]
	*(SC in next 2 rows, skip next row, SC in next row) from*rep to end
	Cut off thread leaving a long tail for sewing

ARMs

Rd 1	**Wheat**: 5SC in magic ring, tighten the ring [5]
Rd 2	INC in each of next 5sts [10]
Rd 3-5	SC in each st around [10] Change to Honey Caramel in last st
	Cut off Wheat
Rd 6-7	**Honey caramel**: SC in each st around [10]
Rd 8	SC BLO in each st around [10]
Rd 9-16	SC in each st around [10]
	Cut off thread leaving a long tail for sewing

HAT DECORATION

STEP 1 BERRIES x3

Rd 1	**Red**: 5SC in magic ring, tighten the ring [5]
Rd 2	INC in each of next 5sts [10]
Rd 3-4	SC in each st around [10]
Rd 5	SC2tog x5 [5] sl st in next st
	Cut off thread leaving a long tail for sewing

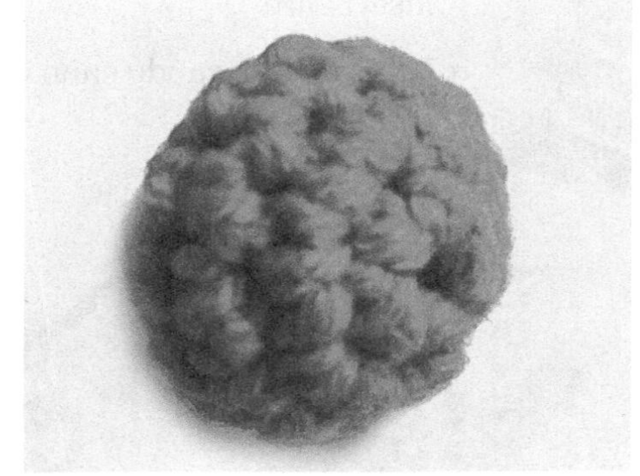

STEP 2 LEAVES Find the leaf pattern on page 18

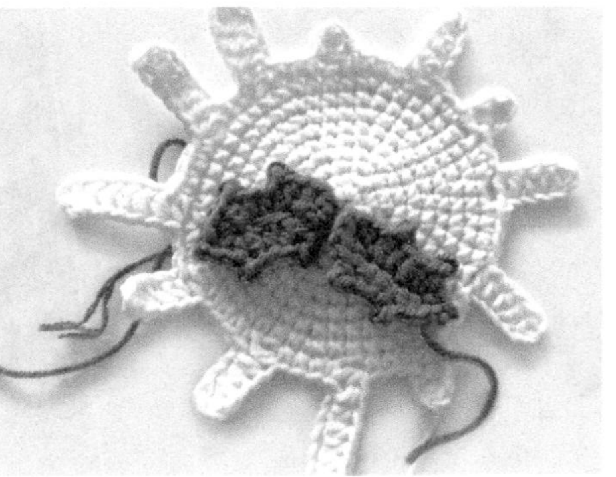

CANDY CANE

Rd 1	**White**: 7SC in magic ring, tighten the ring [7]
NOTE: work all stitches BLO	
Rd 2	SC BLO in each st around. Drop a loop [7]
Rd 3	Step from dropped loop 1 stitch back and work with **Red** SC BLO in next st (pic1,2). Drop the Red loop [7]
NOTE: we work several stitches in white, then drop the white loop and work several stitches in red, then drop a red loop and get back to the white loop again, and so on till we get desired length	
Rd 4	grab the white loop: SC BLO in next 5sts. Drops this loop [7]
Rd 5	Grab the red loop and work SC BLO in next 5sts. Drops this loop...and so on... [7]

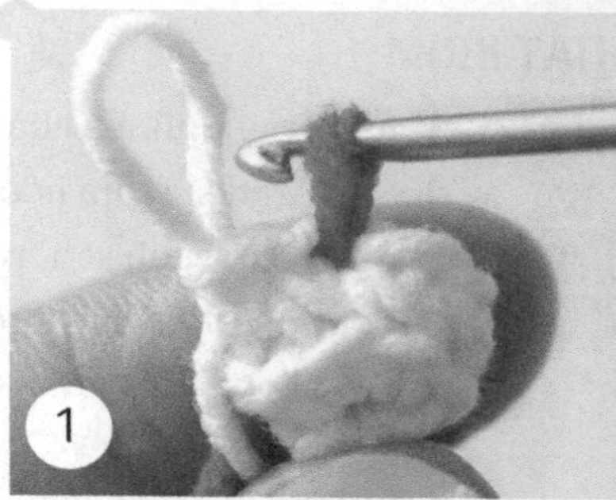
1

2

I have done 26 rounds

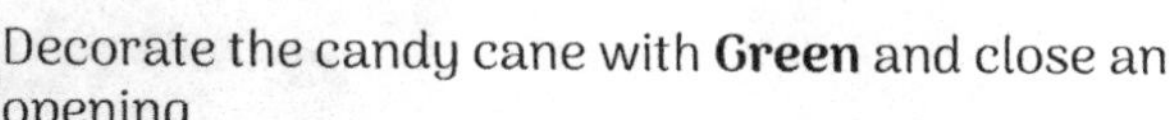

Insert wire

Decorate the candy cane with **Green** and close an opening

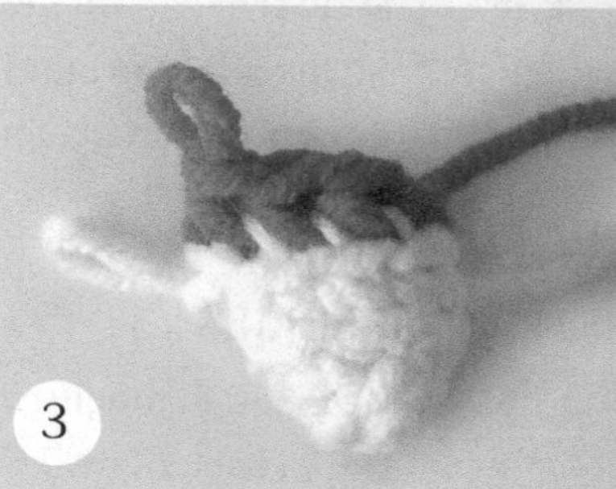
3

4

5

6

7

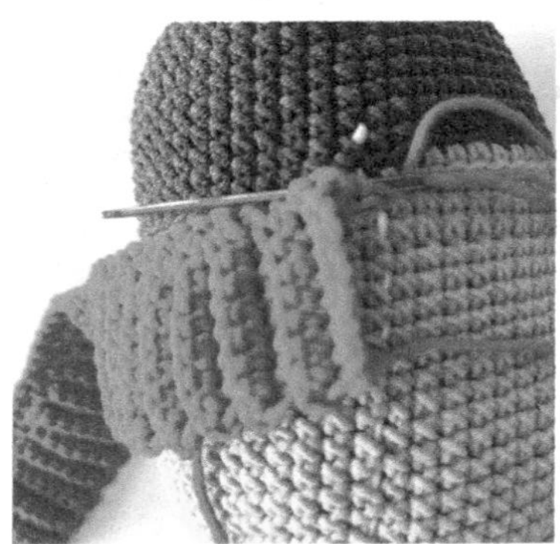

Skip 2 beige rds down from the brown round and sew the beard on the body. Sew the nose on 20th rd of the body.

Sew the hat brim to the brown round of the body starting from the back. When it's done stitch short edges of the brim together.

Result.

Sew or glue the cream topping leaves and berries to the hat.

Stitch one hand to the body to hold the candy cane.

Sew arms to the body under the brim.

Christmas Tree

SIZE: 23 cm / 9 in

	COLOR AND YARN		TOTAL FOR A PROJECT
White		Yarn Art Jeans 62	Approx. 10g/35meters
Bright Green	★	Yarn Art Jeans 52	Approx. 40g/140meters
Wheat	★	Yarn Art Jeans 05	Approx. 10g/35meters

OTHER MATERIALS

- Stuffing approx. 60g

Optional:

- Red wooden bead Ø20mm
- Red ribbon

CROCHET STICHES:

Ch, SC, hdc, DC, INC, sl st, SC2tog, FLO, BLO

ADDITIONAL TOOLS:

Stitch markers x2

Use a contrast thread to mark the beginning of each round.
Do not remove it until your work is completed.

Scan to watch video for Rd 1-21

STEP 1 HAT (WHITE PART)

Rd 1	**White**: 4SC in magic ring, tighten the ring [4]
Rd 2	*(SC in next st, INC in next st)from*rep x2 [6]
Rd 3-4	SC in each st around [6]
Rd 5	INC in each of next 2sts, SC in next 2sts, INC in next st, SC in next st [9]
Rd 6	SC in each st around [9]
Rd 7	SC in next st, INC in each of next 2sts, SC in next 5sts, INC in next st [12]
Rd 8	SC in each st around [12]
Rd 9	SC in next 2sts, INC in each of next 2sts, SC in next 5sts, INC in next st, SC in next 2sts [15]
Rd 10	SC in each st around [15]
Rd 11	SC in next 3sts, INC in each of next 2sts, SC in next 9sts, INC in next st [18]
Rd 12	SC in each st around [18]
Rd 13	SC in next 4sts, INC in each of next 2sts, SC in next 8sts, INC in next st, SC in next 3sts [21]
Rd 14	SC in each st around [21]
Rd 15	SC in next 5sts, INC in each of next 2sts, SC in next 14sts [23]
Rd 16	SC in next 6sts, INC in each of next 2sts, SC in next 14sts, INC in next st [26]
Rd 17	SC in each st around [26]
	Now we work shortened rows
	SC in next 3sts, sl st(place a stitch marker #1 in same stitch as sl st), Turn
	SC in 2nd st from hook, SC in next 2sts, (don't forget to put here your contrast thread-beginning of round), SC in next 10sts, sl st(place a stitch marker #2), Turn
	SC in 2nd st from hook, SC in next 9sts. Do not turn
Rd 18	SC in next 3sts, SC in stitch with a stitch marker #1, SC in next 11 sts, SC in stitch with a stitch marker #2, SC in next 10sts [26]
Rd 19	SC in next 2sts, INC in next st, SC in next 4sts, INC in each of next 2sts, SC in next 7sts, INC in next st, SC in next 9sts [30]
Rd 20	SC FLO in next 3sts, hdc FLO in next 2sts, SC FLO in next 13sts, hdc FLO in next 2sts, DC FLO in next 7sts, hdc FLO in next st, SC FLO in next 2sts [30]

Rd 21	SC in next 3sts, 2hdc in next st, SC in next 14sts, hdc in next 2sts, DC in next 3sts, 2DC in next st, DC in next 3sts, hdc in next st, SC in next 2sts [32]
	Drop a loop (we will use it on step 5 to complete drips). Go to STEP 2

STEP 2 GREEN PART OF THE HAT

Rd 1	Grab the item Right Side Facing, upside down, and join Green to the 1st st of Rd 19 and work into stitches BLO: SC BLO in each st around [30]
Rd 2	*(SC in next 5sts, INC in next st)from*rep x5 [35]
Rd 3-4	SC in each st around [35]
Rd 5	*(SC in next 3sts, INC in next st, SC in next 3sts) from*rep x5 [40]
Rd 6-7	SC in each st around [40]
Rd 8	*(SC in next 7sts, INC in next st)from*rep x5 [45]
Rd 9-11	SC in each st around [45]
Rd 12	*(SC BLO in next 4sts, INC BLO in next st, SC BLO in next 4sts)from*rep x5 [50]
Rd 13-15	SC in each st around [50]
Rd 16	*(SC BLO in next 9sts, INC BLO in next st)from*rep x5 [55]
Rd 17-19	SC in each st around [55]
Rd 20	*(SC BLO in next 5sts, INC BLO in next st, SC in next 5sts) from*rep x5 [60]
Rd 21-22	SC in each st around [60]
Rd 23	SC FLO in each st around [60]
Rd 24	*(SC in next 7sts, INC in next st, SC in next 7sts) from*rep x4 [64]
Rd 25	SC in each st around [64]
Rd 26	*(skip next st, 5DC in next st, skip next st, SC in next st) from*rep x16
	Cut off Green
Rd 27	With a new **White** decorate the edge: slip stitch in each st around
	Cut off thread

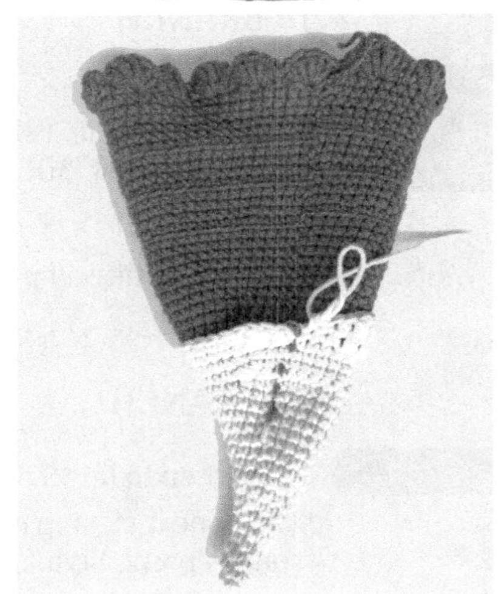

STEP 3 BODY

	Start from Rd 22 and work into stitches BLO with **Green**
Rd 1-2	SC BLO in each st around [60]
Rd 3-9	SC in each st around [60]
Rd 10	*(SC in next 7sts, INC in next st, SC in next 7sts) from*rep x4 [64]
Rd 11-14	SC in each st around [64]
Rd 15	*(SC in next 3sts, SC2tog, SC in next 3sts)from*rep x8 [56]
Rd 16-17	SC in each st around [56]
	Stuff
Rd 18	*(SC in next 5sts, SC2tog)from*rep x8 [48]
Rd 19-20	SC in each st around [48]
Rd 21	SC BLO in each st around [48]
Rd 22	*(SC in next 2sts, SC2tog, SC in next 2sts)from*rep x8 [40]
	Stuff
Rd 23	*(SC in next 3sts, SC2tog)from*rep x8 [32]
Rd 24	*(SC in next st, SC2tog, SC in next st)from*rep x8 [24]
Rd 25	*(SC in next st, SC2tog)from*rep x8 [16]
	Stuff
Rd 26	SC2tog x8 [8]
	Cut off thread and sew the opening

STEP 4 CHRISTMAS TREE BRANCHES

1ST BRANCH

Rd 1	Join **Green** to Rd 19 of STEP 2, work all stitches FLO: *(skip next st, 5DC in next st, skip next st, SC in next st) from*rep x13, skip next st, 5DC in next st, skip next st, sl st in next st
	Cut off thread
Rd 2	With new **White**: slip stitch BLO in each st around.
	Cut off thread

2nd BRANCH

Rd 1	Join **Green** to Rd 15 of STEP 2, work all stitches FLO: *(SC in next st, skip next st, 5DC in next st, skip next st) from*rep x12, SC in next st, sl st.

Cut off thread

Rd 2 With **White**: slip stitch BLO in each st around.

Cut off thread

3rd BRANCH

Rd 1 Join **Green** to Rd 11 STEP 2, work all stitches FLO:
*(skip next st, 5DC in next st, skip next st, SC in next st) from*rep x11, sl st.

Cut off thread

Rd 2 With new **White**: slip stitch BLO in each st around.

Cut off thread

STEP 5 DECORATION ON THE HAT — DRIPS

Get back to STEP 1 — HAT where we left **White**

Continue: make drips:
The first drip is based on a foundation chain 5:
Chain 5, hdc in 2nd Ch from hook, hdc in each st of chain, hdc in stitch of main part where Ch5 comes from, skip next st of a main part (Photo tutorial on page 65), SC in next 1-3 sts of main part to separate drips
The same way we make drips based on different foundation chain lengths and make different number of SC between drips to separate them.

Cut off thread leaving a long tail for sewing.

When your gnome is stuffed sew or glue the drips to give it a neat look.

STEP 6 STAND

Rd 1 With **Green** work FLO into stitches of Rd 19 of STEP 3 (body): Ch1, SC FLO in each st around [48]

Cut off thread

BEARD

Rd 1	**White**: 6SC in magic ring, tighten the ring [6]
Rd 2	SC in each st around [6]
Rd 3	INC in each of next 6sts [12]
Rd 4	SC in next 2sts, 2hdc in each of next 2sts, SC in next 4sts, 2hdc in each of next 2sts, SC in next 2sts [16]
Rd 5	SC in next 3sts, 2hdc in each of next 2sts, SC in next 6sts, 2hdc in each of next 2sts, SC in next 3sts [20]
Rd 6	SC in next 4sts, 2hdc in each of next 2sts, SC in next 8sts, 2hdc in each of next 2sts, SC in next 4sts [24]
Rd 7	SC in next 5sts, 2hdc in each of next 2sts, SC in next 10sts, 2hdc in each of next 2sts, SC in next 5sts [28]
Rd 8	SC in next 6sts, 2hdc in each of next 2sts, SC in next 12sts, 2hdc in each of next 2sts, SC in next 6sts [32]
Rd 9-11	SC in each st around [32]
Rd 12	SC in next 6sts, SC2tog x2, SC in next 12sts, SC2tog x2, SC in next 6sts [28]
Rd 13	SC in next 5sts, SC2tog x2, SC in next 10sts, SC2tog x2, SC in next 5sts [24]
Rd 14	SC in next 4sts, SC2tog x2, SC in next 8sts, SC2tog x2, SC in next 4sts [20]
Rd 15	SC in next 3sts, SC2tog x2, SC in next 6sts, SC2tog x2, SC in next 3sts [16]
	Cut off thread leaving a long tail for sewing.

NOSE

Rd 1	**Wheat**: 6SC in magic ring, tighten the ring [6]
Rd 2	INC in each st around [12]
Rd 3	*(SC in next st, INC in next st)from*rep x6 [18]
Rd 4-5	SC in each st around [18]
Rd 6	*(SC in next st, SC2tog)from*rep x6 [12]
	Cut off thread leaving a long tail for sewing.
	Stuff the nose a bit. Sew or glue the nose to the beard

ARMs

Rd 1	**Wheat**: 5SC in magic ring, tighten the ring [5]
Rd 2	INC in each st around [10]
Rd 3-5	SC in each st around [10] Change to Green in last st
	Cut off Wheat
Rd 6-17	**Green**: SC in each st around [10]
	Cut off thread leaving a long tail for sewing

"If just one person
needs your crochet
work, don't quit.
Even if that person
is you."

Snowman Shortie

SIZE: 16 cm / 6 in

	COLOR AND YARN	TOTAL FOR A PROJECT
Black	Yarn Art Jeans 53	Approx. 15g/55meters
White	Yarn Art Jeans 62	Approx. 20g/70meters
Orange	Yarn Art Jeans 77	Approx. 5g/17meters
Green	Yarn Art Jeans 29	Approx. 7g/25meters
Red	Yarn Art Jeans 90	Approx. 5g/17meters
Dark Brown	Yarn Art Jeans 70	Approx. 10g/35 meters
Yellow	Yarn Art Jeans 58	3g

OTHER MATERIALS

- Stuffing approx. 40g
- Optional: 2 buttons Ø10mm

CROCHET STICHES:

Ch, SC, INC, sl st, SC2tog, FLO, BLO
Surface slip stitch

Use a contrast thread to mark the beginning of each round.
Do not remove it until your work is completed.

STEP 1 HAT

Rd 1	**Black**: 6SC in magic ring, tighten the ring [6]
Rd 2	INC in each st around [12]
Rd 3	*(SC in next st, INC in next st)from*rep x6 [18]
Rd 4	*(SC in next st, INC in next st, SC in next st)from*rep x6 [24]
Rd 5	*(SC in next 3sts, INC in next st)from*rep x6 [30]
Rd 6	*(SC in next 2sts, INC in next st, SC in next 2sts) from*rep x6 [36]
	Check gauge/tension: Ø4.5-5cm
Rd 7	*(SC in next 5sts, INC in next st)from*rep x6 [42]
Rd 8	*(SC in next 3sts, INC in next st, SC in next 3sts) from*rep x6 [48]
Rd 9	*(SC in next 7sts, INC in next st)from*rep x6 [54]
Rd 10	SC BLO in each st around [54]
Rd 11-14	SC in each st around [54]
Rd 15	*(SC in next 8sts, SC2tog, SC in next 8sts)from*rep x3 [51]
Rd 16	SC in each st around [51]
Rd 17	*(SC in next 15sts, SC2tog)from*rep x3 [48] Change to Red in last st
	Leave Black thread on a wrong side
Rd 18-19	**Red**: SC in each st around [48]
	Cut off Red

STEP 2 CONTINUE — HAT BRIM

Rd 20	Grab **Black**: *(SC FLO in next 7sts, INC FLO in next st) from*rep x6 [54]
Rd 21	*(SC in next 4sts, INC in next st, SC in next 4sts) from*rep x6 [60]
Rd 22	*(SC in next 9sts, INC in next st)from*rep x6 [66]
Rd 23	*(SC in next 5sts, INC in next st, SC in next 5sts) from*rep x6 [72]
Rd 24	*(SC in next 11sts, INC in next st)from*rep x6 [78]
Rd 25	sl st BLO in each st around [78]
	Cut off thread

STEP 3 DECORATION ON A BRIM

Rd 1	With **Red**: surface slip stitch in between of Rd 17 and Rd 18;
Rd 2	surface slip stitch sl st in each sts of Rd 19 and Rd 20
	Cut off thread

STEP 4 BODY

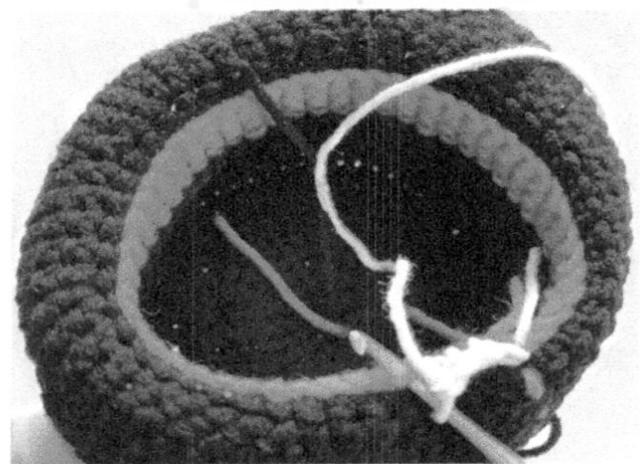

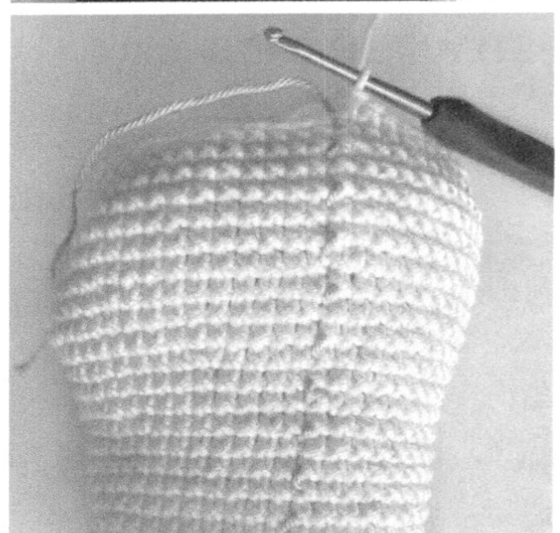

Rd 1	Grab a hat upside down and work into stitches BLO of Rd 19 STEP 1 with **White**: SC BLO in each st around [48]
Rd 2-8	SC in each st around [48]
Rd 9	SC in next 11sts, SC BLO in next 3 sts(we will attach the arm to these sts), SC in next 20sts, SC BLO in next 3sts, SC in next 11sts (we will attach the arm to these sts)[48]
Rd 10	SC in each st around [48]
Rd 11	*(SC in next 7sts, INC in next st)from*rep x6 [54]
Rd 12-13	SC in each st around [54]
Rd 14	*(SC in next 4sts, INC in next st, SC in next 4sts) from*rep x6 [60]
Rd 15-16	SC in each st around [60]
Rd 17	*(SC in next 9sts, INC in next st)from*rep x6 [66]
Rd 18-21	SC in each st around [66]
Rd 22	*(SC in next 9sts, SC2tog)from*rep x6 [60]
Rd 23	SC in each st around [60]
Rd 24	*(SC in next 4sts, SC2tog, SC in next 4sts) from*rep x6 [54]
Rd 25	SC in each st around [54]
Rd 26	*(SC in next 7sts, SC2tog)from*rep x6 [48]
Rd 27	SC BLO in each st around [48]
Rd 28	*(SC in next 3sts, SC2tog, SC in next 3sts)from*rep x6 [42]
Rd 29	SC in each st around [42]
Rd 30	*(SC in next 5sts, SC2tog)from*rep x6 [36]
	Stuff
Rd 31	*(SC in next 2sts, SC2tog, SC in next 2sts)from*rep x6 [30]
Rd 32	*(SC in next 3sts, SC2tog)from*rep x6 [24]
Rd 33	*(SC in next st, SC2tog, SC in next st)from*rep x6 [18]
Rd 34	*(SC in next st, SC2tog)from*rep x6 [12]
	Stuff well
Rd 35	SC2tog x6 [6]
	Cut off thread and sew the opening

STEP 5 STAND

With a new **White** work into stitches of Rd 26 of the body: Ch1, SC FLO in each st around [48]
Cut off thread

STEP 6 FRAME BUCKLE

Yellow: Embroider a frame buckle

SCARF

	Light green: Chain 6 [6]
Row 1	SC in 2nd st from hook, SC in next 4sts [5]Ch1, Turn
Row 2-29	SC BLO in each st around [5]Ch1, Turn
Row 30	SC BLO in each st around [5]

Fold in half and stitch short edges together by SC on a wrong side.

Cut off thread and weave in

STICKS

STEP 1 LONG STICK

Rd 1	**Dark Brown**: 6SC in magic ring, tighten the ring [6]
Rd 2-5	SC in each st around [6]
Rd 6	SC in each st to last st [6] sl st in next st

Cut off thread

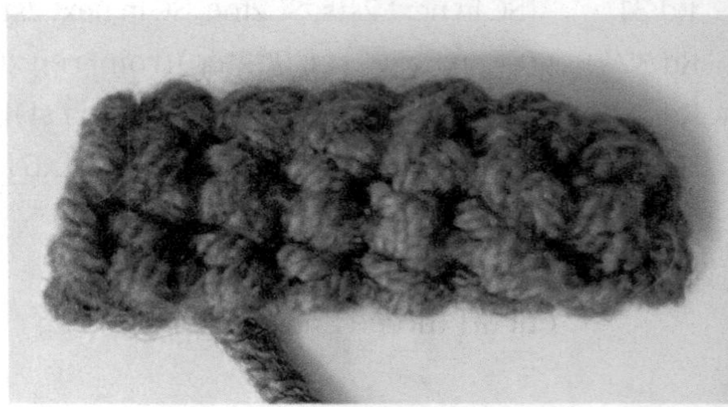

STEP 2 SHORT STICK

Rd 1	**Dark Brown**: 6SC in magic ring, tighten the ring [6]
Rd 2-3	SC in each st around [6]
	Do not cut off thread and go to the next step

STEP 3 ASSEMBLE

Arrange together the long and the short sticks as illustrated in mage below

Insert your hook through stitches of both fabrics and make SC.

Make SC in next 3 stitches the same way.

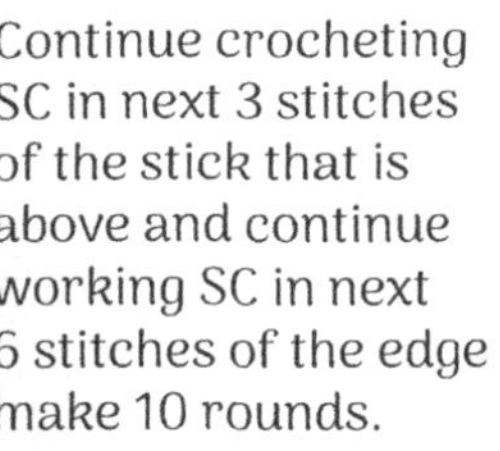

Continue crocheting SC in next 3 stitches of the stick that is above and continue working SC in next 6 stitches of the edge make 10 rounds.

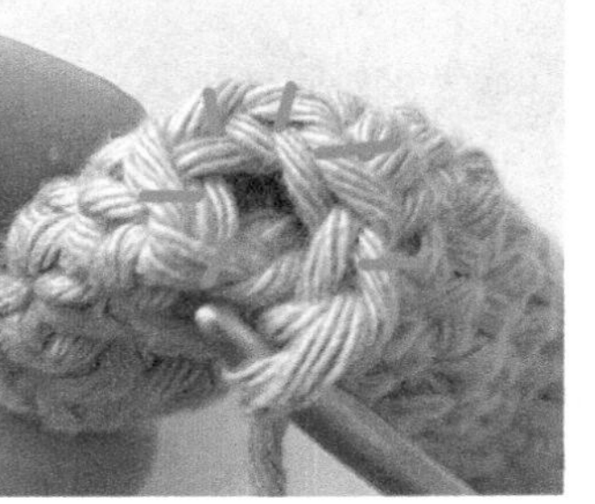

NOSE

Rd 1	**Orange**: 6SC in magic ring, tighten the ring [6]
Rd 2	INC in each st around [12]
Rd 3	*(SC in next st, INC in next st) from*rep x6 [18]
Rd 4-5	SC in each st around [18]
Rd 6	*(SC in next st, SC2tog) from*rep x6 [12]

Cut off thread leaving a long tail for sewing.

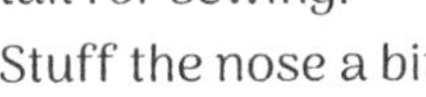

Stuff the nose a bit

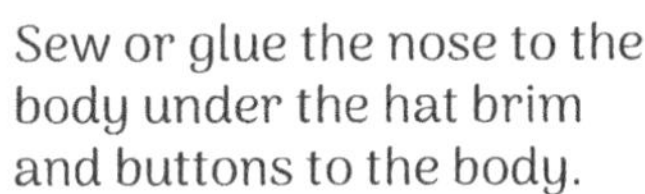

Sew or glue the nose to the body under the hat brim and buttons to the body.

Sew on the arms to stitches FLO of Rd 8 of the body.

Put the scarf on your Snowman.

Mrs. Santa Claus

SIZE: 20 cm / 8 in

	COLOR AND YARN	TOTAL FOR A PROJECT
Fog Grey	Yarn Art Jeans 49	Approx. 15g/50meters
White	Yarn Art Jeans 62	Approx. 10g/35meters
Honey Caramel	Yarn Art Jeans 07	Approx. 10g/35meters
Green	Yarn Art Jeans 69	Approx. 6g/20meters
Red	Yarn Art Jeans 90	Approx. 20g/70meters

OTHER MATERIALS

- Stuffing approx. 40g
- Optional: Wire for an eyeglass or a ready toy eyeglass
- Button x1

CROCHET STICHES:

Ch, SC, hdc, DC, INC, sl st, SC2tog, FLO, BLO

Use a contrast thread to mark the beginning of each round. Do not remove it until your work is completed.

STEP 1 HEAD

Rd 1	**Fog Grey**: 6SC in magic ring, tighten the ring [6]
Rd 2	INC in each st around [12]
Rd 3	*(SC in next st, INC in next st)from*rep x6 [18]
Rd 4	*(SC in next st, INC in next st, SC in next st) from*rep x6 [24]
Rd 5	*(SC in next 3sts, INC in next st)from*rep x6 [30]
Rd 6	SC in each st around [30]
Rd 7	*(SC in next 2sts, INC in next st, SC in next 2sts) from*rep x6 [36]
Rd 8	*(SC in next 5sts, INC in next st)from*rep x6 [42]
Rd 9	SC in each st around [42]
Rd 10	*(SC in next 3sts, INC in next st, SC in next 3sts) from*rep x6 [48]
Rd 11-20	SC in each st around [48]
Rd 21-22	Ch2, hdc FLO in next 21sts, SC FLO in next 2sts, sl st in next st, SC FlO in next 2 sts, hdc FLO in next 21sts, sl st in Ch2 of rd[48]
Rd 23	sl st in each st around [48]
	Surface slip stitches in stitches of Rd 21 [48]
	Surface slip stitches in stitches of Rd 22 [48]
	Cut off thread

STEP 2 BUN

Rd 1	**Grey**: 7SC in magic ring, tighten the ring [7]
Rd 2	INC BLO in each st around [14]
Rd 3	*(SC BLO in next st, INC BLO in next st) from*rep x7 [21]
Rd 4	*(SC BLO in next st, INC BLO in next st, SC BLO in next st) from*rep x7 [28]

Rd 5	*(SC BLO in next 3sts, INC BLO in next st) from*rep x7 [35]
Rd 6-7	hdc BLO in each st around [35]
	Cut off thread leaving a long tail for sewing.
	Sew the bun on the head by tapestry needle to stitches of Rd 7 HEAD. Stuff it as you work

STEP 3 BODY

Rd 1-2	**Red: work into stitches BLO of Rd 20 of STEP** SC BLO in each st around [48]
Rd 3-9	SC in each st around [48]
Rd 10	*(SC in next 7sts, INC in next st)from*rep x6 [54]
Rd 11	SC in each st around [54]
Rd 12	SC BLO in each st around [54]
Rd 13	SC in each st around [54]
Rd 14	*(SC in next 4sts, INC in next st, SC in next 4sts) from*rep x6 [60]
Rd 15-16	SC in each st around [60]
Rd 17	*(SC in next 13sts, SC2tog)from*rep x4 [56]
Rd 18-19	SC in each st around [56]
Rd 20	*(SC in next 5sts, SC2tog)from*rep x8 [48]
Rd 21-22	SC in each st around [48]
Rd 23	SC BLO in each st around [48]
Rd 24	*(SC in next 2sts, SC2tog, SC in next 2sts) from*rep x8 [40]
	Stuff the hat
Rd 25	*(SC in next 3sts, SC2tog)from*rep x8 [32]
Rd 26	*(SC in next st, SC2tog, SC in next st) from*rep x8 [24]
Rd 27	*(SC in next st, SC2tog)from*rep x8 [16]
	Stuff
Rd 28	SC2tog x8 [8]
	Cut off thread and sew the opening

RED BOW

STEP 1 MAIN PART

	Red: Foundation chain: Chain 13 [13]
Row 1	SC in 2nd stitch from hook, SC in next 11sts [12]
Row 2-10	Ch1, SC BLO in each st across [12]

Tie the middle of the bow with a long thread. Leave long ends to tie on the bun

STEP 2

	Green: Foundation chain: Chain 9 [9]
Row 1	sl st in 2nd stitch from hook, sl st in next 7sts [8]

Cut off thread leaving a long tail for sewing. Sew the bow base to the bow. Tie a bow to the hair bun

NOSE

	Honey Caramel Foundation chain: Chain 4 [4]
Rd 1	3SC in 2nd stitch from hook, SC in next st, 3SC in last st of chain, in bottom the foundation chain: SC in next st [8]
Rd 2	INC in each of next 3sts, SC in next st, INC in each of next 3sts, SC in next st [14]
Rd 3-4	SC in each st around [14]

Cut off thread leaving a long tail for sewing. Sew the nose under the hair starting from Rd 1 Body

ARMs

STEP 1 PALMS

Rd 1	**Honey Caramel**: 5SC in magic ring, tighten the ring [5]
Rd 2	INC in each st around [10]
Rd 3-5	SC in each st around [10] Change to Red in last st
	Cut off Honey Caramel
Rd 6-7	**Red**: SC in each st around [10]
Rd 8	SC BLO in each st around [10]
Rd 9-17	SC in each st around [10]
	Cut off thread

STEP 2 CUFF

Rd 1	With **White** work into stitches FLO of Rd 7: SC FLO in each st around [10]
Rd 2-3	SC in each st around [10]
	Cut off thread

SKIRT

STEP 1 SKIRT

	■ **Green**: Foundation chain: Chain 63 and join in round by sl st in first Ch [64]
	Use a tapestry crochet technique to make the skirt (see page 107)
Rd 1-3	Ch1, *(■ **Green**: SC in next 4sts, ■ **Honey Caramel**: SC in next 4sts) from*rep x7, ■ **Green**: SC in next 4 sts, ■ **Honey Caramel**: SC in next 3 sts, sl st in 1st st of rd (Note: In 3rd Round complete last sl st with ■ **Red**) [64]
Rd 4-6	Ch1, *(■ **Red**: SC in next 4sts, ■ **Green**: SC in next 4sts) from*rep x7, ■ **Red**: SC in next 4 sts, ■ **Green**: SC in next 3 sts, sl st in 1st st of rd [64] (Note: In 6th Round complete last sl st with ■ **Green**)
Rd 7-9	Ch1, *(■ **Green**: SC in next 4sts, ■ **Honey Caramel**: SC in next 4sts)from*rep x7, ■ **Green**: SC in next 4sts, ■ **Honey Caramel**: SC in next 3 sts, sl st in 1st st of rd [64]

(Note: In 9th Round complete last sl st with **Red**)

Rd 10	Ch1, *(■ **Red**: SC in next 4sts, ■ **Green**: SC in next 4sts)from*rep x7, ■ **Red**: SC in next 4 sts, ■ **Green**: SC in next 3 sts, sl st in 1st st of rd [64]
Rd 11	**White**: *(Ch2, sl st in next st) all in one stitch repeat around
	Cut off threads

STEP 2 APRON

Row 1	**White**: 5SC in magic ring, tighten the ring, Turn [5]
Row 2	Ch1, INC in each of next 5sts, Turn [10]
Row 3	Ch1, SC in each st across, Turn [10]
Row 4	Ch1, *(SC in next st, INC in next st)from*rep x5, Turn [15]
Row 5	Ch1, SC in each st across, Turn [15]
Row 6	*(4DC in next st, skip next st, sl st in next st) from*rep x5 Cut off thread

STEP 3 ASSEMBLE

1. With **White**: Chain 30 (1st strap),
2. Join the chain to a skirt waistband to the beginning of the round by slip stitch and work sl st into next 24 stitches of the skirt edge
3. Join the apron to the skirt by 10 SC inserting your hook through both fabrics
4. Continue working sl st into edge stitches to last 4 stitches
5. Chain 30 (2nd strap)
6. Cut off thread

Sew the arms on the body.

Sew or glue the button.
Put the skirt on Mrs. Santa Claus.

SHOES

Rd 1	**Red**: 6SC in magic ring, tighten the ring [6]
Rd 2	INC in each st around [12]
Rd 3	*(SC in next st, INC in next st)from*rep x6 [18]
Rd 4-6	SC in each st around [18]
Rd 7	*(SC in next st, SC2tog) from*rep x6 [12] Stuff a bit. Stitch edges together by SC closing the opening. Sew to the loops of Rd 22

EYEGLASSES

"The older we get, the shorter our
Christmas wish lists become and
what we find is that what we want
isn't something that money can buy."

Grandpa Santa

SIZE: 23 cm / 9 in

	COLOR AND YARN	TOTAL FOR A PROJECT
Fog Grey	Yarn Art Jeans 49	Approx. 10g/35meters
White	Yarn Art Jeans 62	Approx. 2g/7meters
Honey Caramel	Yarn Art Jeans 07	Approx. 15g/50meters
Red	Yarn Art Jeans 90	Approx. 20g/70meters
Black	Yarn Art Jeans 53	Approx. 7g/25meters
Yellow	Yarn Art Jeans 58	Approx. 0.5g

OTHER MATERIALS

- Stuffing approx. 40g
- Optional: Wire for an eyeglass or a ready toy eyeglass

+ stitch marker x1

CROCHET STICHES:

Ch, SC, hdc, DC, INC, sl st, SC2tog, FLO, BLO

Use a contrast thread to mark the beginning of each round.
Do not remove it until your work is completed.

STEP 1 HEAD

Rd 1	**Honey Caramel**: 6SC in magic ring, tighten the ring [6]
Rd 2	INC in each st around [12]
Rd 3	*(SC in next st, INC in next st)from*rep x6 [18]
Rd 4	*(SC in next st, INC in next st, SC in next st) from*rep x6 [24]
Rd 5	*(SC in next 3sts, INC in next st)from*rep x6 [30]
Rd 6	SC in each st around [30]
Rd 7	*(SC in next 2sts, INC in next st, SC in next 2sts) from*rep x6 [36]
Rd 8	*(SC in next 5sts, INC in next st)from*rep x6 [42]
Rd 9	SC in each st around [42]
Rd 10	*(SC in next 3sts, INC in next st, SC in next 3sts) from*rep x6 [48]
Rd 11-20	SC in each st around [48] Change to Red in last st Cut off Honey Caramel

STEP 2 CONTINUE BODY

Rd 21-22	**Red**: SC BLO in each st around [48]
Rd 23-27	SC in each st around [48]
Rd 28	*(SC in next 7sts, INC in next st)from*rep x6 [54]
Rd 29-31	SC in each st around [54]
Rd 32	*(SC in next 4sts, INC in next st, SC in next 4sts) from*rep x6 [60]
Rd 33-34	SC in each st around [60]
	Place a stitch marker to the last stitch of Rd34 to mark a belt
Rd 35	SC BLO in each st around [60]
Rd 36	*(SC in next 14sts, INC in next st)from *rep x4 [64]
Rd 37-38	SC in each st around [64]
Rd 39	*(SC in next 3sts, SC2tog, SC in next 3sts) from*rep x8 [56]
Rd 40-41	SC in each st around [56]
Rd 42	*(SC in next 5sts, SC2tog)from*rep x8 [48]
Rd 43-44	SC in each st around [48]
Rd 45	SC BLO in each st around [48]
Rd 46	*(SC in next 2sts, SC2tog, SC in next 2sts) from*rep x8 [40]

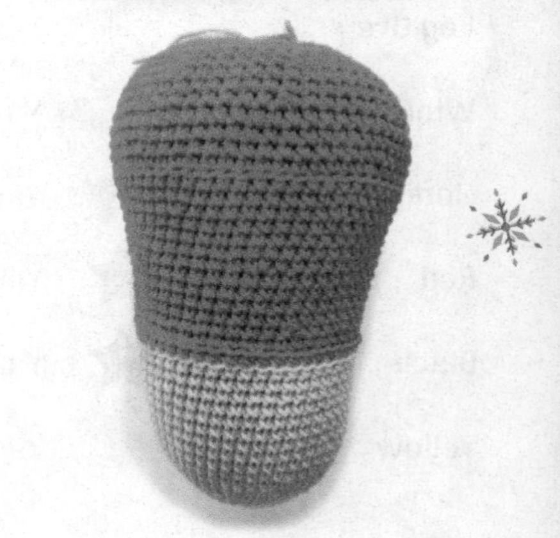

Stuff

Rd 47 *(SC in next 3sts, SC2tog)from*rep x8 [32]

Rd 48 *(SC in next st, SC2tog, SC in next st)from*rep x8 [24]

Rd 49 *(SC in next st, SC2tog)from*rep x8 [16]

Stuff

Rd 50 SC2tog x8 [8]

Cut off thread and sew the opening

STEP 3 HEM

Rd1 Join new **Red** to stitch with the marker: Ch2, DC FLO in next 27sts, hdc FLO in next st, SC FLO in next st, sl st FLO in next st (place a stitch marker into this stitch), SC FLO in next st, hdc FLO in next st, DC FLO in next 27 sts, sl st in 2nd Ch [60]

Cut off thread

Rd 2 Join **White**: (sl st in next st, Ch1)in each st around [120]

Cut off thread

IMITATION OF A BUTTON PLACKET ON THE COAT

Join **White** To the stitch with the stitch marker: Chain 12 [12]

Cut off thread. We will fix this chain later

BELT

Black: Foundation chain: Chain 62 [62]

Row 1 DC in 4th stitch from hook, DC in each st to end [60]

Cut off thread. Sew or glue the belt to the waist

With **Yellow** embroider a frame buckle

BEARD

The beard consists of 5 parts. We are going to crochet each part separately and then join them together

STEP 1 PART #1

Rd 1	**Fog Grey**: 6SC in magic ring, tighten the ring [6]
Rd 2	INC in each st around [12]
Rd 3-5	SC in each st around [12]
	Cut off thread

STEP 2, 3 PART #2, #4

Rd 1	**Fog Grey**: 6SC in magic ring, tighten the ring [6]
Rd 2	INC in each st around [12]
Rd 3	*(SC in next 5sts, INC in next st)from*rep x2 [14]
Rd 4-6	SC in each st around [14]
	Cut off thread

STEP 4 PART #3

Rd 1	**Fog Grey**: 6SC in magic ring, tighten the ring [6]
Rd 2	INC in each st around [12]
Rd 3	*(SC in next 3sts, INC in next st)from*rep x4 [16]
Rd 4-7	SC in each st around [16]
	Cut off thread

STEP 5 PART #5

Rd 1	**Fog Grey**: 6SC in magic ring, tighten the ring [6]
Rd 2	INC in each st around [12]
Rd 3-5	SC in each st around [12]
	Do not cut off thread. Go to STEP 6

STEP 6 ASSEMBLE

Rd 1	Arrange all parts 1-2-3-4-5 as illustrated in the image and join then working in edge stitches (pic.1). SC in next 6sts of the part#1, SC in next 7sts of the part# 2 (pic.2). SC in next 8sts of the part#3 (pic.3), SC in next 7sts of the part#4, SC in next 12sts of the part#5 (pic.4), SC in next 7sts of the part #4, SC in next 8sts of the part #3, SC in next 7sts of the part #2, SC in next 6sts of the part #1
Rd 2	SC2tog, SC in next 4 sts, SC2tog, SC in next 5sts, SC2tog, SC in next 6sts, SC2tog, SC in next 5sts, SC2tog, SC in next 4sts, SC2tog, SC in next 4sts, SC2tog, SC in next 5sts, SC2tog, SC in next 6sts, SC2tog, SC in next 5sts, SC2tog, SC in next 4sts [58]. Stuff this detail a little bit (pic.5)

Row 3	Now we are going to work through both sides of the beard edge stitching edges together and closing the opening: *(SC in next 4 stitches, then SC-2tog of a front layer and skip 2sts accordingly of the back layer)from*rep x2; SC in next 5 stitches, then SC2tog of a front layer and skip 2sts accordingly of the back layer, SC in next 4 stitches, then SC2tog of a front layer and skip 2sts accordingly of the back layer, SC in next 4 stitches.

Cut off thread leaving a long tail for sewing (pic.6)

NOSE

	Honey Caramel: Foundation chain: Chain 4 [4]
Rd 1	3SC in 2nd stitch from hook, SC in next st, 3SC in last st of the foundation chain, in bottom of chain: SC in next st [8]
Rd 2	INC in each of next 3sts, SC in next st, INC in each of next 3sts, SC in next st [14]
Rd 3-4	SC in each st around [14]

Cut off thread leaving a long tail for sewing. Sew the nose to the part #3 of the beard

Attach the beard to the last round of the head

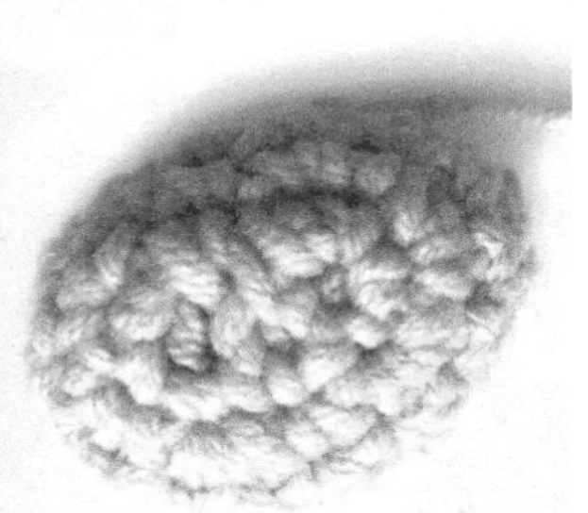

ARMs

STEP 1 ARM

Rd 1	**Honey Caramel**: 5SC in magic ring, tighten the ring [5]
Rd 2	INC in each st around [10]
Rd 3-5	SC in each st around [10]Change to Red in last st
	Cut off Honey Caramel
Rd 6-7	**Red**: SC in each st around [10]
Rd 8	SC BLO in each st around [10]
Rd 9-17	SC in each st around [10]

Cut off thread leaving a long tail for sewing

STEP 2 CUFF

Rd 1	With **White** work into stitches of Rd 7: SC FLO in each st around [10]
Rd 2-3	SC in each st around [10]
	Cut off thread

BOOTS

Rd 1	**Black**: 6SC in magic ring, tighten the ring [6]
Rd 2	INC in each st around [12]
Rd 3	*(SC in next st, INC in next st)from*rep x6 [18]
Rd 4-6	SC in each st around [18]
Rd 7	*(SC in next st, SC2tog)from*rep x6 [12]

Cut off thread leaving a long tail for sewing.

Stuff a bit. Stitch edges together by SC closing the opening. Sew to the loops of Rd 44 Body

HAT

STEP 1 HAT

Rd 1	**Red**: 6SC in magic ring, tighten the ring [6]
Rd 2	*(SC in next st, INC in next st)from*rep x3 [9]
Rd 3	SC in each st around [9]
Rd 4	*(SC in next st, INC in next st, SC in next st) from*rep x3 [12]
Rd 5	SC in each st around [12]
Rd 6	*(SC in next st, INC in next st, SC in next st) from*rep x4 [16]
Rd 7	SC in each st around [16]
Rd 8	*(SC in next 3sts, INC in next st)from*rep x4 [20]
Rd 9	SC in each st around [20]

Rd 10	*(SC in next 2sts, INC in next st, SC in next 2sts) from*rep x4 [24]
Rd 11	SC in each st around [24]
Rd 12	*(SC in next 5sts, INC in next st)from*rep x4 [28]
Rd 13	SC in each st around [28]
Rd 14	*(SC in next 3sts, INC in next st, SC in next 3sts) from*rep x4 [32]
Rd 15	SC in each st around [32]
Rd 16	*(SC in next 7sts, INC in next st)from*rep x4 [36]
Rd 17	SC in each st around [36]
Rd 18	*(SC in next 4sts, INC in next st, SC in next 4sts) from*rep x4 [40]
Rd 19	SC in each st around [40]
Rd 20	*(SC in next 9sts, INC in next st)from*rep x4 [44]
Rd 21	SC in each st around [44]
Rd 22	*(SC in next 5sts, INC in next st, SC in next 5sts) from*rep x4 [48]
Rd 23-24	SC in each st around [48]
Rd 25	*(SC in next 11sts, INC in next st)from*rep x4 [52]
Rd 26-27	SC in each st around [52]
Rd 28	*(SC in next 6sts, INC in next st, SC in next 6sts) from*rep x4 [56]
Rd 29-30	SC in each st around [56]
Rd 31	*(SC in next 13sts, INC in next st)from*rep x4 [60]
Rd 32-36	SC in each st around [60] Change to White in last st
	Cut off Red
Rd 37-41	**White**: SC in each st around [60]
	Cut off thread

STEP 2 POMPON

Rd 1	**White**: 5SC in magic ring, tighten the ring [5]
Rd 2	INC in each st around [10]
Rd 3	*(SC in next st, INC in next st)from*rep x5 [15]
Rd 4-5	SC in each st around [15]
Rd 6	*(SC in next st, SC2tog)from*rep x5 [10]
	Cut off thread. Sew the opening and sew the pompon to a hat top.

Embroider several stitches to imitate the hair and make a forelock.
Make eyeglasses of a wire and put on Grandpa.

EYEGLASSES

Scan for the video tutorial

Lady Gnome

SIZE: 24cm/10in

	COLOR AND YARN	TOTAL FOR A PROJECT
Red	★ Yarn Art Jeans 90	Approx. 25g/80meters
Grey	★ Yarn Art Jeans 46	Approx. 20g/70meters
Wheat	★ Yarn Art Jeans 05	Approx. 7g/25meters
White	Yarn Art Jeans 62	Approx. 12g/40meters

OTHER MATERIALS

- Stuffing approx. 40g
- Optional: a green bead Ø12mm; a green ribbon

CROCHET STICHES:

Ch, SC, INC, sl st, SC2tog, FLO, BLO, surface slip stitch

NOTE: When change a yarn cut off if it's stated in a pattern in other cases, drop a yarn and raise when it's needed

STEP 1 HAT

Rd 1	**Red**: 6SC in magic ring, tighten the ring [6]
Rd 2-7	SC in each st around [6]
Rd 8	*(SC in next st, INC in next st)from*rep x3 [9]
Rd 9-12	SC in each st around [9]
Rd 13	*(SC in next st, INC in next st, SC in next st) from*rep x3 [12]
Rd 14-16	SC in each st around [12]
Rd 17	*(SC in next 3sts, INC in next st)from*repx3 [15]
Rd 18-20	SC in each st around [15]
Rd 21	*(SC in next 2sts, INC in next st, SC in next 2sts) from*rep x3 [18]
Rd 22-24	SC in each st around [18]
Rd 25	*(SC in next 5sts, INC in next st)from*rep x3 [21]
Rd 26-28	SC in each st around [21]
Rd 29	*(SC in next 3sts, INC in next st, SC in next 3sts) from*rep x3 [24]
Rd 30-32	SC in each st around [24]
Rd 33	*(SC in next 7sts, INC in next st)from*rep x3 [27]
Rd 34-36	SC in each st around [27]
Rd 37	*(SC in next 4sts, INC in next st, SC in next 4sts) from*rep x3 [30]
Rd 38-40	SC in each st around [30]
Rd 41	*(SC in next 9sts, INC in next st)from*rep x3 [33]
Rd 42-44	SC in each st around [33]
Rd 45	*(SC in next 5sts, INC in next st, SC in next 5sts) from*rep x3 [36]
Rd 46-48	SC in each st around [36]
Rd 49	*(SC in next 11sts, INC in next st)from*rep x3 [39]
Rd 50-51	SC in each st around [39]
Rd 52	*(SC in next 6sts, INC in next st, SC in next 6sts) from*rep x3 [42]
Rd 53-54	SC in each st around [42]
Rd 55	*(SC in next 13sts, INC in next st)from*rep x3 [45]
Rd 56-57	SC in each st around [45]
Rd 58	*(SC in next 7sts, INC in next st, SC in next 7sts) from*rep x3 [48]

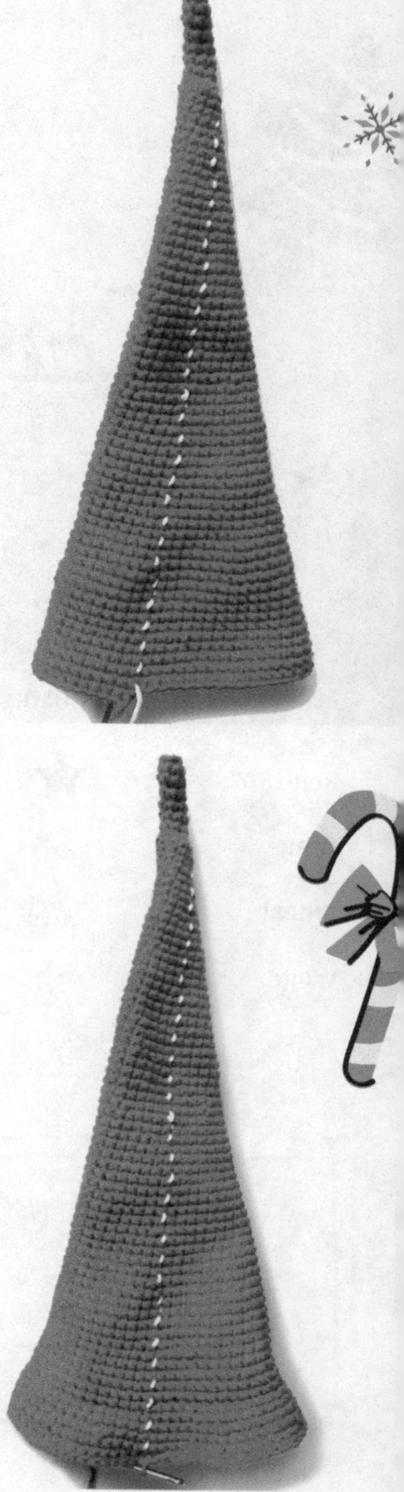

Rd 59-60	SC in each st around [48]
Rd 61	*(SC in next 15sts, INC in next st)from*rep x3 [51]
Rd 62-63	SC in each st around [51]
Rd 64	*(SC in next 8sts, INC in next st, SC in next 8sts) from*rep x3 [54]
Rd 65	SC in each st around [54]

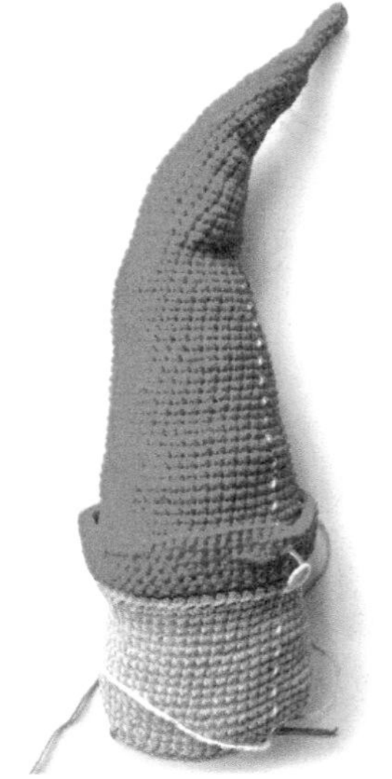

STEP 2 CONTINUE – HAT BRIM

Rd 66	SC FLO in each st around [54]
Rd 67	*(SC in next 4sts, INC in next st, SC in next 4sts) from*rep x6 [60]
Rd 68	*(SC in next 7sts, INC in next st, SC in next 7sts) from*rep x4 [64]
Rd 69	*(SC in next 15sts, INC in next st)from*rep x4 [68]
Rd 70	*(SC in next 8sts, INC in next st, SC in next 8sts) from*rep x4 [72]
Rd 71	slip stitch in each st around [72]
	Cut off thread

STEP 3 BODY

Rd 1-2	Grab the hat upside down and with **Grey** work into Rd 65 BLO: SC BLO in each st around [54]
Rd 3-6	SC in each st around [54]
Rd 7	*(SC in next 4sts, INC in next st, SC in next 4sts) from*rep x6 [60]
Rd 8-11	SC in each st around [60]
Rd 12	*(SC in next 7sts, INC in next st, SC in next 7sts) from*rep x4 [64]
Rd 13-14	SC in each st around [64]
Rd 15	*(SC in next 3sts, SC2tog, SC in next 3sts) from*rep x8 [56]
Rd 16-18	SC in each st around [56]
	Stuff the hat
Rd 19	*(SC in next 5sts, SC2tog)from*rep x8 [48]
Rd 20-21	SC in each st around [48]
Rd 22	SC BLO in each st around [48]
Rd 23	*(SC in next 2sts, SC2tog, SC in next 2sts) from*rep x8 [40]
	Stuff
Rd 24	*(SC in next 3sts, SC2tog)from*rep x8 [32]
Rd 25	*(SC in next st, SC2tog, SC in next st)from*rep x8 [24]

Rd 26	*(SC in next st, SC2tog)from*rep x8 [16]
	Stuff
Rd 27	SC2tog x8 [8]
	Cut off thread and sew the opening

STEP 3 STAND

Rd 1	With a new **Grey** work into stitches of Rd 22 of the body: Ch1, SC FLO in each st around [48]
	Cut off thread

STEP 4 DECORATION

Rd 1	With **Red** work surface slip stitches in between Rd 17 and 18 around
	Cut off thread

NOSE

Rd 1	**Wheat**: 6SC in magic ring, tighten the ring [6]
Rd 2	INC in each st around [12]
Rd 3	*(SC in next st, INC in next st)from*rep x6 [18]
Rd 4-5	SC in each st around [18]
Rd 6	*(SC in next st, SC2tog)from*rep x6 [12]
	Cut off thread leaving a long tail for sewing. Stuff the nose a bit. Attach to the body under the hat brim.

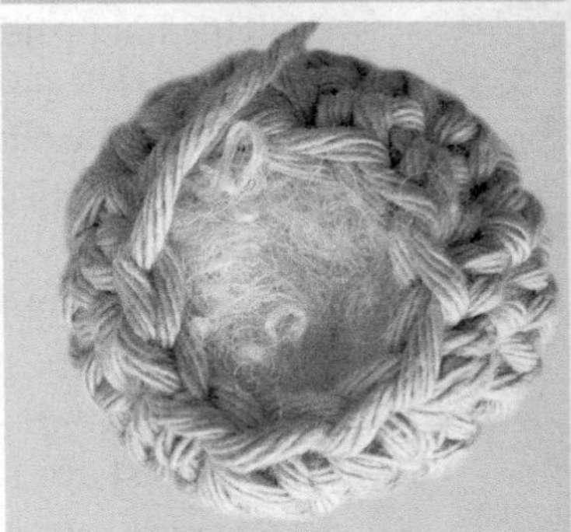

ARMs

STEP 1 PALM

Rd 1	**Wheat**: 5SC in magic ring, tighten the ring [5]
Rd 2	INC in each st around [10]
Rd 3-5	SC in each st around [10] Change to Grey in last st. Cut off Wheat
Rd 6-7	**Grey**: SC in each st around [10]
Rd 8	SC BLO in each st around [10]
Rd 9-17	SC in each st around. Cut off thread [10]
	Cut off thread

STEP 2 CUFF

Rd 1	With new **Red** work into stitches of Rd 7: SC FLO in each st around [10]
Rd 2	SC in each st around [10]
	Cut off thread

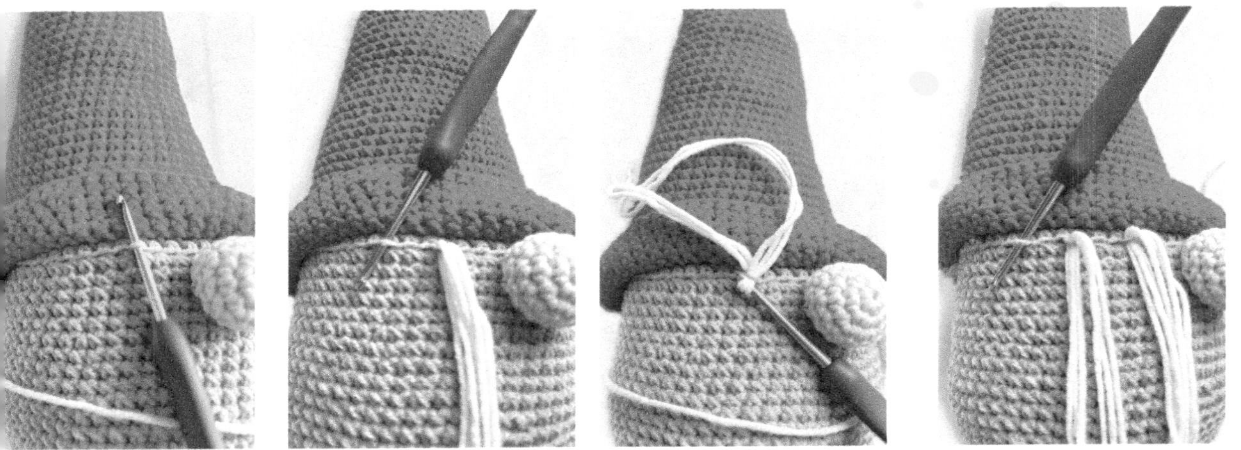

ach (sew on/glue) the nose to the body and make braids.

Attach the arms to the body and decorate the hat with a green bead and a ribbon.

Abbreviations (US terms)

St(s)	Stitch/es
Rd	Round
Ch	Chain stitch
SC	**Single Crochet "V" and "X"** The typical method to make a single crochet is to insert your hook into a stitch, yarn over, pull through, yarn over, pull through both loops. This method makes a 'V' stitch. The other lesser-known method to make a single crochet is to insert your hook into a stitch, yarn under, pull through, yarn over, pull through both loops. This method makes an 'X' stitch. Please, note that I use SC "x".
DC	Double Crochet: yarn over, insert hook in stitch, yarn over, pull through stitch, [yarn over, pull through two loops] twice
sl st	slip stitch: insert hook in stitch, yarn over, pull through both loops on hook
hdc	Half Double Crochet: yarn over, insert in stitch, yarn over, pull through st, yarn over, pull through all 3 loops on hook
TR	Triple crochet: Yarn over the hook 2 times and insert your hook in indicated stitch. Yarn over the hook and pull hook through stitch. Yarn over the hook and draw your yarn through the first 2 loops on your hook. Yarn over the hook and draw your yarn through the next 2 loops on your hook. Yarn over the hook and draw your yarn through the last 2 loops on your hook.
SC2tog	Single crochet two together: Insert hook into stitch and draw up a loop. Insert hook into next stitch and draw up a loop. Yarn over, draw through all 3 loops on hook.
INC	Increase: single crochet in one stitch twice
Ch-space	Chain-space

Scan for the video tutorial

Abbreviations (US terms)

prev	previous
BLO	Back loop only
FLO	Front Loop only
*(...)from*rep x	work instructions within parentheses as many times as directed by x
Surface slip stitch	Place a thread behind the fabric, insert hook into the crocheted fabric from the front to the back and grab yarn on hook, pull a loop through to the front. Insert hook from front to back and pull a loop to the front side and through the loop on the front of the fabric to create a surface slipped stitch.

COLOR CHANGING AND TAPESTRY CROCHET

Tapestry crochet: Crochet as usual with the non-working color carried inside the stitch.

Color changing you follow the pattern until it is time to switch colors, in the stitch previous to the new color, complete the final yarn over and draw through with the new color you are switching to. **Always change color in the last stitch of a current color completing the last stitch with a new color.**

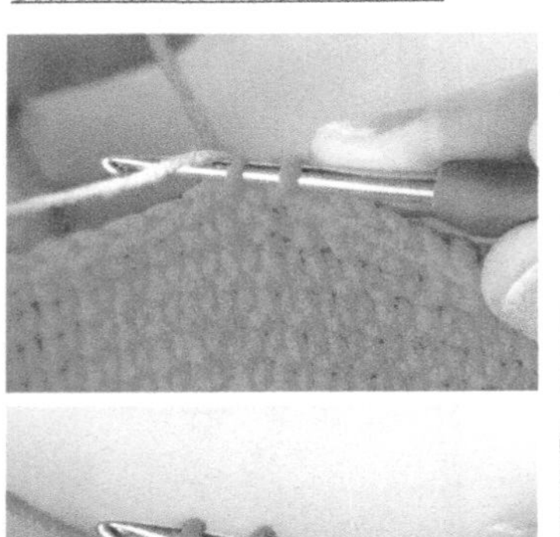
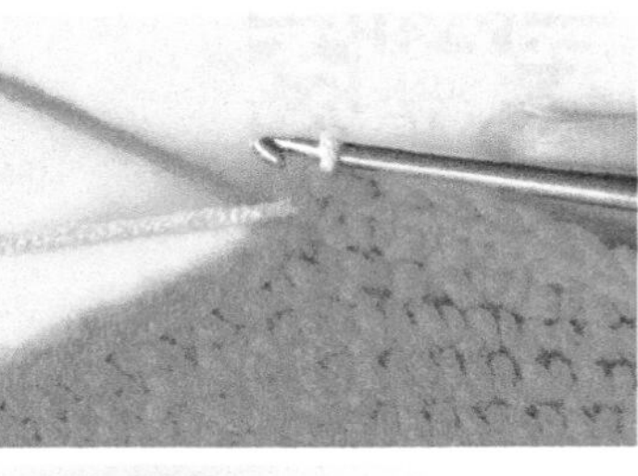
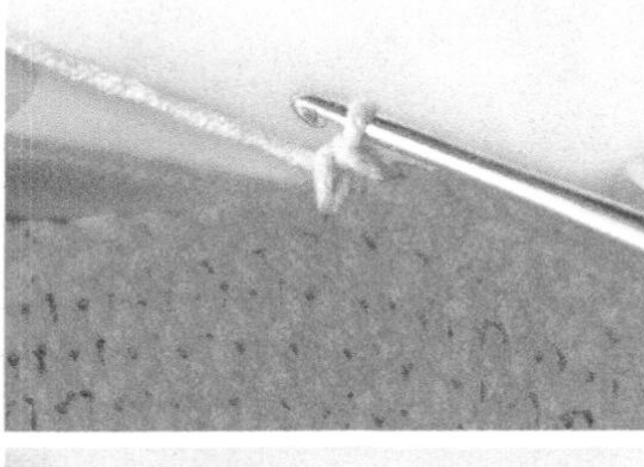

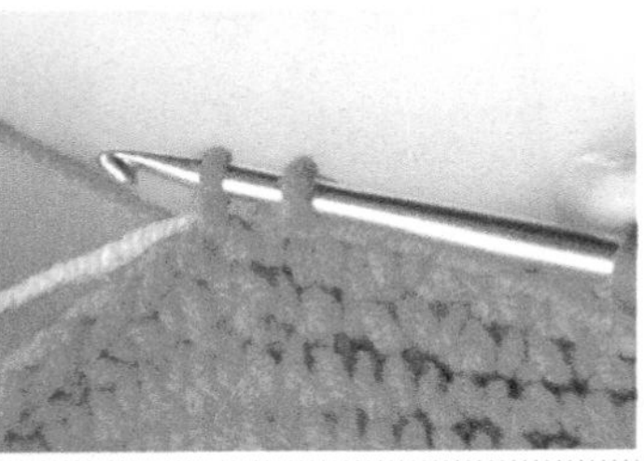

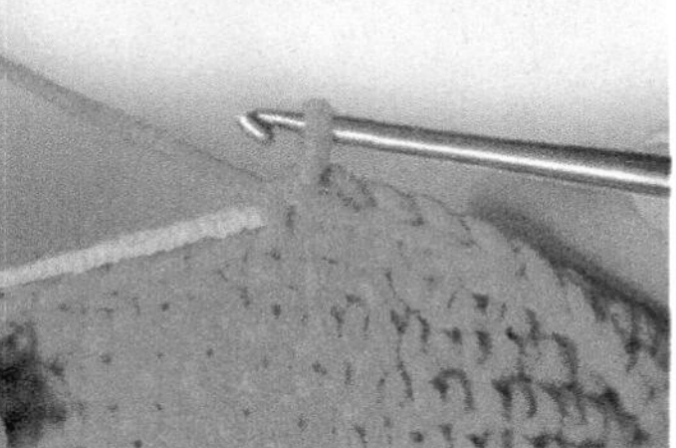

INVISIBLE FINISH FOR OPEN CROCHET EDGES

MAGIC RING

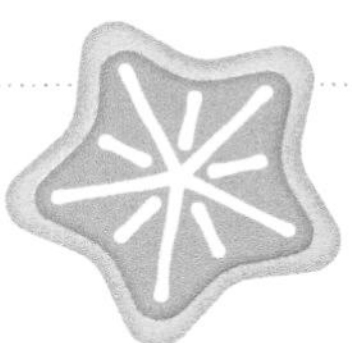

More crochet gnomes patterns, inspiration, social media
Find here

Made in the USA
Las Vegas, NV
28 September 2023